The Story
of the Mass

From the Last Supper
to the Present Day

Pierre Loret, C.SS.R.

Foreword by
Archbishop Rembert G. Weakland

Translated by
Dorothy Marie Zimmerman, S.S.N.D.
Adapted for North American readers by
Roger Marchand

LIGUORI
PUBLICATIONS

One Liguori Drive
Liguori, Missouri 63057
(314) 464-2500

Imprimi Potest:
John F. Dowd, C.SS.R.
Provincial, St. Louis Province
Redemptorist Fathers

Imprimatur:
Monsignor Edward J. O'Donnell
Vicar General, Archdiocese of St. Louis

This book is a translation of *La Messe du Christ à Jean-Paul II, Histoire de la liturgie Eucharistique,* published by Editions Salvator, Mulhouse, France.

ISBN 0-89243-171-7
Library of Congress Catalog Card Number: 82-83984

Liguori Publications thanks the following publishers
for the use of material quoted from:

THE ANTE-NICENE FATHERS, Vol. I and VII, Wm. B. Eerdmans Publishing Co., Grand Rapids, Michigan. Reprinted 1975. Used by permission.

The NEW AMERICAN BIBLE, copyright © 1970, by the Confraternity of Christian Doctrine, Inc. Washington, D.C. Used by permission. All rights reserved.

THE MASS OF THE ROMAN RITE, by Josef A. Jungmann, S.J. Published by Benziger, Division of Glencoe Publishing Co., Inc., Encino, California. Copyright © 1951. Used by permission.

THE DOCUMENTS OF VATICAN II, Abbott-Gallagher edition. Published by America Press, Inc., New York, New York. Copyright © 1966. Used by permission. All rights reserved.

Excerpts from VATICAN COUNCIL II: THE CONCILIAR AND POST CONCILIAR DOCUMENTS, edited by Austin Flannery, O.P., copyright © 1975, used by permission of Costello Publishing Co., Northport, N.Y. 11768.

Cover design by Pam Hummelsheim

Contents

Foreword by Archbishop Rembert G. Weakland, O.S.B. . . . . ⁊

Foundation Chapter: The Mass of Christ 9

Part One
The Mass in Early Christianity
(From the Last Supper to A.D. 604)

1 The Mass in the Time of the Apostles 18
2 The Mass in the Time of the Persecutions 29
3 The Golden Age of the Eucharistic Liturgy 44

Part Two
The Mass in the Middle Ages
(A.D. 604 to A.D. 1517)

4 The Dialogue Between Rome and Gaul 60
5 Roman Tradition and the Carolingian Renaissance 69
6 The Gothic Mass 81

Part Three
The Mass in the Modern Era
(A.D. 1517 to the Present Day)

7 The Mass of Saint Pius V 90
8 From the Council of Trent to Vatican II 101
9 The Choice of Vatican II and the Missal of Paul VI 113

Conclusion:
Pope John Paul II on Eucharistic Renewal 133

Index of Names and Subjects 138

In this 250th anniversary year
of the Redemptorist Congregation,
this book is dedicated to
Saint Alphonsus Liguori,
lover of the Eucharist,
founder of the Redemptorists;
and to Francis A. Brunner,
Redemptorist priest, liturgist,
who translated into English
Josef A. Jungmann's *Missarum Sollemnia*.

FOREWORD

It often has been said that the people were not properly prepared for the liturgical renewal of the Second Vatican Council. That was so, of course, because neither were the bishops, priests, and religious educators. What was most lacking on the part of all — and especially here in the United States — was a sense of history. Liturgy had been seen as a set of immutable rubrics, divinely inspired and divinely transmitted. The multiple sources and the many factors that brought into being our liturgy before Vatican II were not generally known. If only Father Loret's book had been written in 1964 and had become a part of a mandated reading list for all Catholics!

Father Pierre Loret, C.SS.R., has written a history of the Mass for everyone. That is, indeed, a brave undertaking. Many scholars will criticize the book for being too simple and unnuanced, some will say it does not incorporate scholarship since the time of Josef Jungmann (whose monumental work appeared in German in 1948), some will say that at times it seems more apologetical than historical; but I am sure all will agree that the risk had to be taken and that Father Loret has succeeded well.

The liturgical renewal of Vatican II was well prepared by scholars and particular groups. Intensified historical studies and monographs had been appearing in scholarly journals since the last century. They were written for the most part by Benedictine monks, forced in the period of monastic restoration in the 19th century to record the roots of their spirituality. These studies had led to practical, pastoral results in the liturgical movements that swept Europe and the United States before and after the Second World War. Nevertheless, knowledge of this renewal was still limited to experts before the Council. The Council made it the living heritage of all Catholics.

Father Loret's book should be of help to all members of parish liturgy committees, to priests and laity alike. Most of all, it should aid all Catholics, and especially those who struggle to comprehend the liturgical changes brought about by the Second Vatican Council, to see that the reforms we now enjoy are rooted in history and form a part of the glorious Tradition of the Church. The liturgical renewal will be seen, then, as a restoration of the finest of the Catholic Tradition — not for the sake of archaeological purity, but for the spiritual benefit of all believers.

+ Rembert G. Weakland

Most Reverend Rembert G. Weakland, O.S.B.
Archbishop of Milwaukee

Foundation Chapter:
The Mass of Christ

Jesus did not give a name to what he did at the Last Supper on the eve of his Passion. The only term the Gospels give for that first Eucharist is "this" — "Do *this* as a remembrance of me" (Luke 22:19).

The term *Mass* made its appearance only in the fourth century A.D., and it did not really become widespread until the fifth and sixth centuries. But recent historians — for example, Josef Jungmann, S.J., in his masterful work, *The Mass of the Roman Rite* — have called the Last Supper "the first holy Mass."[1] Taking that phrase as its cue, this chapter is entitled "The Mass of Christ."

The First Mass

Jesus lived a simple, poor life. Sometimes, as night began to fall, he did not even have anywhere "to lay his head," no home to welcome him.

But for this one Passover, *his* Passover, Jesus ordered special arrangements. He told two of his disciples: *"Go into the city and you will come upon a man carrying a water jar. Follow him. Whatever house he enters, say to the owner, 'The Teacher asks, Where is my guest room where I may eat the Passover with my disciples?' Then he will show you an upstairs room, spacious, furnished, and all in order. That is the place you are to get ready for us."* (Mark 14:13-15; Luke 22:10-12)

That is how Jesus conveyed the importance of what he was about to do — that is, institute "the Mass." Let us pay close attention; what we have here is the basis and point of departure for the whole history of the Eucharist throughout the ages.

Jesus and his disciples arrive at the chosen house. It is evening. Everything is ready. Jesus is solemn but happy, overflowing with love. He confides to his disciples: *"I have greatly desired to eat this Passover with you before I suffer."* (Luke 22:15)

The apostles are keenly aware that this Passover is like no other. It is a key moment in human history. But they apparently draw a false conclusion from their awareness. They see this moment as a chance to get front seats for themselves in the Kingdom of God, and start bickering about who will be closest to the Master!

Jesus is saddened by this display. It is their last evening with him, and his followers still do not understand his way of humility and love.

Silently, Jesus rises, takes a towel, and like a household slave, begins to wash their feet. The apostles watch in shocked amazement as Jesus attends to them, one by one.

When he has washed the last foot, Jesus finally speaks. It is the apostles' turn to be silent as he asks:

"Do you understand what I just did for you?"

They remain silent, unsure of what to say. That the washing was important, they have no doubt; Jesus has just told Peter, *"If I do not wash you, you will have no share in my heritage."* But now Jesus has a second lesson he wants to impress on them. He says: *"But if I washed your feet — I who am Teacher and Lord — then you must wash each other's feet. What I just did was to give you an example, as I have done, so you must do."* (John, chapter 13)

In centuries to come, disputes between "disciples" would take place regarding the Eucharist. What Jesus began at the Last Supper as a source of love between him and his friends has sometimes become an occasion of division and even hatred. But that is not what Jesus intended. At the Supper we have just witnessed in our minds, Jesus took bread in his hands and it became his Body. He took a cup of wine and the wine became his Blood. He then invited his disciples to eat his Body and drink his Blood. He sacrificed himself for his own and gave himself to them as food. It was his supreme moment of humble, self-giving love — the first Mass.

What Was Received and Passed On

In the Last Supper scene described above, you may have noticed that there is no mention of the words Jesus spoke when he changed bread and wine into his Body and Blood. Why the omission?

From a twentieth-century viewpoint, you might expect a historian to focus on the exact words of Christ that are at the very heart of the Eucharistic liturgy. After all, don't the Gospels give us Jesus' own words?

The answer to that question is not quite as simple as many people think.

To begin with, there are two kinds of testimony that are passed down in history — *written* and *oral* testimony. In some cultures, even today, oral testimony predominates.

Oral, word-of-mouth testimony can be very *literal* and unchanging, as in the case of famous quotations. For example, Patrick Henry's "Give me liberty or give me death" has been passed on unchanged for centuries. But more frequently, oral tradition is *free*. That is, it communicates the substance of the original facts or sayings, but it does so freely, in a variety of forms. This second, freer mode of tradition is the way in which the sayings, stories, and deeds of Jesus were passed on before they were written down in the New Testament — and this includes the accounts of the first Eucharist.

A prime example of testimony received and passed on is Saint Paul's account of Jesus' words at the Last Supper. In the eleventh chapter of 1 Corinthians, Paul says: *"I received from the Lord what I handed on to you, namely, that the Lord Jesus on the night he was betrayed took bread. . . ."* (11:23)

What Paul is handing on in this passage, he received in a privileged, inner way from the risen Lord. But the human words that Paul transmits in writing came to him from earlier, oral testimony of others in the Christian community.

We who live in the twentieth century might wish that a reporter had tape-recorded the voice of Jesus and photographed that historic moment. But such a "freezing" of his words and gestures is not what Jesus had in mind. He did not even have a secretary on hand taking notes of the event. In fact, the first testimony we have of Jesus' words at the Last Supper — in chapter 11 of 1 Corinthians — was not written down until about twenty years afterwards. And in that testimony the words of Jesus were not reported in the language in which Jesus spoke them — Aramaic, most likely — but in Greek. We do not know the exact words Jesus spoke at the Last Supper. Nor do we know the exact order in which he spoke them.

If Jesus had wanted to pass on a strict, literal transcript of his words at the Last Supper, he would have done so — and we would be celebrating the Mass today in Aramaic, the language he spoke. But that was not the Lord's intention. What he gave us is the testimony of the early community — *"Whoever hears you, hears me."* He did not say "Re*tell* this," tying us to an exact set of words; he gave us the words *"Do* this," binding us to the deep meanings of the action he performed.

We have access to the words and actions of Jesus only through translations from ancient traditions and editors (the evangelists). We can, of course, try to reconstruct what Jesus said in his mother tongue. Such reconstructions give us only probabilities, not certainties, about what Jesus actually said. But at the same time, they are a sure source of what Jesus *meant*. Let us take a look at four of them — the testimonies of the New Testament writers.

Jesus' Foundational Words

The following chart groups the New Testament witnesses two by two according to their similarities. Luke is paired with Paul, and Matthew with Mark. The lineup shows variations as well as similarities.

Each of the four witnesses reports Jesus saying "THIS IS MY BODY." The statement is so brief and striking that it is difficult to imagine that it has undergone any change. The Mark-Matthew form of the statement leaves out the rest of what is said over the bread, as if to highlight the force of the basic statement.

PAUL in A.D. 56	LUKE circa A.D. 80
"THIS IS MY BODY which is for you. Do this in remembrance of me … after the supper … This CUP is the new COVENANT in MY BLOOD."	"THIS IS MY BODY to be given for you. Do this as a remembrance of me. … after the supper … This CUP is the new COVENANT in MY BLOOD, which will be shed for you."
MARK circa A.D. 65	MATTHEW circa A.D. 75-80
"Take this, THIS IS MY BODY. He likewise took a CUP . . . THIS IS MY BLOOD, the blood of the COVENANT, to be poured out on behalf of many."	"Take this and eat it, THIS IS MY BODY. Then he took a cup … THIS IS MY BLOOD, the blood of the COVENANT, to be poured out in behalf of many for the forgiveness of sins."

In regard to the CUP, all four testimonies speak of BLOOD and of COVENANT. They express the meaning, but do it in a free, not a literal, way. Paul and Luke say: "COVENANT in MY BLOOD." Mark and Matthew say: "MY BLOOD of the COVENANT." Matthew's version is the longest.

In each case there is fidelity to the meaning of the words, without slavish literalness.

So from the beginning — in the biblical testimonies themselves — there was variety in the ritual formulas of the Mass. And yet, all four witnesses are inspired by one same Spirit — the Spirit of Christ. No one's testimony can be said to be demonstrably more traditional or more authentic than the others'.

Here we see God's "style" of revealing. God does not send magic formulas down from heaven; what we receive are the responsible testimonies of disciples freely welcoming God's SPIRIT.

It should come as no surprise, then, to read the following from the French scholar, Father Jounel:

"In the various liturgies of the Eastern and Western churches — apart from those of the Reformed churches — H. Leclerc collected no less than eighty-five different wordings of the narrative of the institution of the Mass. Not one version reproduced literally the text of any of the synoptic Gospels or of Saint Paul."[2]

It is also instructive to note that the "formula of consecration" in the missal of Pope Saint Pius V, which for centuries was the only one allowed in the Latin Church, is not rigorously identical to any one of the four in the New Testament.

In our own time, the missal of Pope Paul VI gives us new variations of the four Last Supper narratives. In one way or another, each of the New Testament narratives draws a connection between the Last Supper and Jesus' Passion. So do the texts in the new missal.

When Jesus said "This is my body" and "This is my blood," he was not uttering words to be repeated as if they were a magic formula. His words are the remembrance of an act of love, a sacrament that draws us into the mystery of his broken Body, his Blood poured out. . . .

Notes

1. See Josef A. Jungmann, *The Mass of the Roman Rite,* Volume One, page 7 (Benziger Brothers, Inc., 1950).
2. See Pierre Jounel, ''La composition des nouvelles prières eucharistiques,'' *La Maison-Dieu* 94, 1968, page 43.

PART ONE
The Mass in Early Christianity
(From the Last Supper to A.D. 604)

1 The Mass in the Time of the Apostles

2 The Mass in the Time of the Persecutions

3 The Golden Age of the Eucharistic Liturgy

1
The Mass in the Time of the Apostles

The four Evangelists — Matthew, Mark, Luke, and John — tell us that Jesus instituted the Eucharist. But it is Saint Paul's first letter to Corinth, and the sequel to Luke's Gospel — Acts of the Apostles — that give us an idea of what the Mass was really like in the days of the apostles.

Within a few short years, Christian liturgy evolved into something unique and original. Paul and Luke disclose the profound changes the Eucharistic liturgy underwent during the apostles' lifetime. This was a key period in the history of the Mass.

The Responsibility of the Apostles

After the death of Jesus, the apostles were helpless. They had lost their bearings. Here they were in a hostile atmosphere, having lost all hope of a messianic renewal. As the apostles huddled together behind locked doors, even the apparitions of the risen Christ seem only to have increased their fear of Jesus' enemies.

But then, with the coming of the Holy Spirit at Pentecost, the apostles were transformed. They regained their courage and once again showed themselves in public. They even addressed the crowds, proclaiming that Jesus Christ is our only salvation. (Read Acts of the Apostles, chapter 2.)

In those days, what was the "Mass" like?

The apostles had the Master's instruction: "Do this as a remembrance of me." But exactly how to carry out this mandate was completely up to them. The memorial would undoubtedly be a rite. But would it be celebrated once a year like the Passover, or oftener? According to what rhythm, what ceremonial pattern? Matters such as these had to be worked out.

Among the apostles there were no Jewish priests, no Levites, no leader of a synagogue. The apostles' experience was that of heads of families, called upon to preside at the Passover meal and at family Sabbath suppers, meals which had a religious orientation. In the following years, the apostles' pioneering efforts would be the source of liturgical change and development throughout the centuries. The Church did not receive a ready-made Eucharistic liturgy. Its task was to give the Mass form and expression in each ensuing age.

As might be expected, the apostles began their Eucharistic worship maintaining a liturgical bond with the Jewish Temple which, in his lifetime, Jesus had frequented.

A Twofold Liturgy

The apostles and their newly baptized converts frequented the Temple. On returning home, however, they would begin a second liturgy. Luke tells us: *"They went to the temple area together every day, while in their homes they broke bread"* (Acts 2:46 — In Saint Luke's writings the "breaking of bread" refers to the Eucharist).

For how long a time did the disciples of Jesus practice this twofold liturgy? We do not know. The decision to break away from the Temple seems to have been imposed on the apostles by the Jewish leaders. These leaders had arrested and maltreated the apostles and had stoned Stephen, the first Christian martyr. A youth named Saul, who was too young to take part in Stephen's execution, guarded the cloaks of the men who did the stoning. (Read Acts 6:8 to 8:3.) Only a few years later this Saul, more than any other person, would bring about the complete break between Jewish and Christian liturgies.

The Intervention of Saul...Become Paul

Saul was a man to be reckoned with. He was a devout Pharisee and a careful scholar. He was also a man who harbored deep feelings against the disciples of Christ, whom he considered traitors against the Jewish nation. But then came the personal intervention of Christ — Saul's experience of Jesus on the road to Damascus — and Saul became Christ's total apostle.

Saul would willingly have sacrificed himself for the salvation of his brother Jews. But most Jews found his message intolerable. Saul was consumed with this vision: the true Messiah is Christ; it is in him alone that Jews and pagans alike must seek salvation. In every town or city he entered, Saul would first direct his steps to the local synagogue. Time after time the synagogue would reject his overtures. Sick at heart, Saul would then shake the dust from his sandals and go away.

On the island of Cyprus he changed his name from the Jewish name *Saul* to the Roman name *Paul*. This name-change was significant. With Paul and through Paul, Christian liturgy would henceforth come into its own and define its most characteristic features. Let us look at the most obvious of those features.

The Basis of Sharing in Liturgy

Only true Jews may participate in Jewish liturgy. In the Temple, Jews have a court reserved for them; any non-Jew daring to venture there would risk maltreatment. Paul was falsely accused of having transgressed the law, and the crowd rose up against him. Luke depicts the scene: *"They seized him, shouting: 'Fellow Israelites, help us! This is the man who . . . has even brought Greeks into the temple area and thus profaned this sacred place.'"* They dragged Paul outside the Temple and immediately closed its gates. The mob tried to kill Paul. When word reached the Roman cohort, the troop commander took his soldiers and charged into the crowd of rioters, saving Paul's life. (Acts 21:27-32)

The sign of entry into the Jewish people is circumcision, which concerns only males. In the Temple there is an outer court reserved for men. Women have a separate court of their own. Women can be present at synagogue worship, but they cannot take an active part in it. So there is a stark contrast between the conditions for taking part in Jewish and Christian worship. For participation in even the heart of Christian liturgy — the breaking of bread — there is only one condition. One need not belong to a particular people or race, or be male or female. One need only be baptized. Baptism may be conferred on any human being, the sole requirement being that the request for it be sincere. Whoever receives Baptism enters into the Christian people on an equal footing with all. Paul is very explicit on this point. He says: *"All of you who have been baptized into Christ have clothed yourselves with him. There does not exist among you Jew or Greek, slave or freeman, male or female. All are one in Jesus Christ."* (Galatians 3:27-28)

In contrast, no unbaptized person can participate fully in the breaking of bread regardless of national or family background.

The Shift to Christian Liturgy

Was there, then, no need for Jewish rites and liturgy in order to become a disciple of the Jew named Jesus? No, replied Paul. There is not.

Today, twenty centuries later, that change in thinking hardly makes an impact on us. But for Jewish converts to Christianity, the shock caused by Paul's insight was profound. Even the apostles were divided on the issue. For Paul the matter was clear: universal Christian reality and the future of the Christian message were in jeopardy. In the end, Peter and the other apostles were won over to Paul's way of thinking. (Read Paul's letter to the Galatians, chapter 2, and Acts of the Apostles, chapter 15.)

In the beginning, Christians attended worship in the Temple of Jerusalem, which included its sacrificial rites. These sacrifices were the *raison d'être* for the Temple. One could pray officially in the synagogues, but it was only in the Temple that sacrifices were offered.

Meanwhile, the Christians were also "breaking bread in their homes." They perceived this rite as a "sacrifice" in which the Lamb of God offers himself to glorify his Father and to save the people, his brothers and sisters.

This shift was revolutionary. The Christians had passed beyond the gory, spectacular sacrifices of the Temple. As peaceful and subdued as it was, the Christians' sacrifice liturgy was a deeply realistic one because it gave them a way of sharing in the sacrifice of the Cross.

The Switch from Saturday to Sunday

By the time Paul's first letter to the Corinthians and Luke's Acts of the Apostles were composed, Christian liturgical meetings were being held on the first day of the week — Sunday. (See 1 Corinthians 16:2 and Acts 20:7.) For Jews, the day of worship was the Sabbath — Saturday. When did the Christians make the switch from Saturday to Sunday? We do not know the exact date. But we do know some of the reasons for the change. It was on the evening of this "first day" of the New Creation — Sunday — that the risen Jesus again shared a meal with his disciples. One week later he repeated that act, this time with Thomas present. (Read John 20:19-29.) Here we see the Sunday-to-Sunday rhythm of Jesus' memorial meal reflected in the Gospel.

The Language Used in Liturgy

At the Passover meal, Jesus most probably used his mother tongue, Aramaic. Just as Jewish Christians in Israel spoke Aramaic, Christians in Greek-speaking nations spoke Greek. To the apostles, the use of one's own language in the liturgy was taken for granted. Paul, too, took it for granted. As early as the year 56, Paul wrote the following about those who were inspired by the Spirit to speak in mysterious tongues: *"Thank God, I speak in tongues more than any of you, but in the church I would rather say five intelligible words to instruct others than ten thousand words in a tongue."* (1 Corinthians 14:18-19)

The first language change, then, was from the original

Aramaic to Greek, the language spoken by most of the early Christians. The preference was for understandable language in the liturgy. This preference caused no uproar, a fact which argues that intelligible language in liturgy was regarded as essential during that foundation period.

The "Breaking of the Bread" Becomes Ritualized

The various sacrificial rites of the Temple, and their accompanying prayers, were performed according to time-honored prescriptions. This, however, was not the case with the early Eucharist. All that the Christians had to go by, originally, were the words and actions of Christ when he changed bread and wine into his Body and Blood.

Certain liturgical habits or rituals were soon established, however. Several of these rituals appeared in writing by the spring of A.D. 56, in the account of the Last Supper in chapter 11 of Paul's first letter to Corinth. For example, Paul twice says *"Do this . . . in remembrance of me"* (in verses 24 and 25) and *"whenever you drink"* and *"every time . . . you eat this bread and drink this cup"* (in verses 25 and 26). Such words and phrases differ from Paul's usual vocabulary, leading scholars to think that they are formulas which Paul is repeating from an already established tradition.[1]

Does the breaking of the bread have to be ritualized as an actual meal, or is a meal simply the natural setting in which this memorial takes place? Whatever the case, tension developed early between the attitude of some of the meal guests and the memorial it celebrates.

In chapter 11 of 1 Corinthians, Paul writes: *"What I have to say is not said in praise, because your meetings are not profitable but harmful. . . . When you assemble it is not to eat the Lord's Supper, for everyone is in haste to eat his own supper. One person goes hungry while another gets drunk"* (verses 17, 20, and 21).

From this passage we learn that the "breaking of the bread" took place during, or on the occasion of, a meal. We also see that these get-togethers did not always turn out to be religious experiences.

Were the disorders Paul attacked symptoms of a split between the Eucharist and a domestic meal? Perhaps so. Writing roughly ten and twenty years later, Mark and Matthew lead us to suspect that, by that time, the "breaking of the bread" in their communities no longer took place in the course of a meal. In Paul's account, the two consecrations are separated; the consecration of the bread takes place during the supper, and the consecration of the wine "after the supper." But in later accounts (Mark 14:22-24 and Matthew 26:26-28) the two consecrations take place one after the other, with no meal in between.

In any case, the Eucharist was evolving, freeing itself from the setting of a meal. Sitting down to an actual meal soon became secondary; the sharing of the bread and wine came to be seen as the true sacrificial meal.

The Structure of the Mass: the Liturgy of the Word

Why does the Mass have a liturgy of the Word before the sharing of the bread and wine? And where did this liturgy of the Word come from?

The answer is simple, and it clearly shows the link between Christian and Jewish prayer.

In the days of the apostles, the liturgy of the synagogue began with readings from the Law and the Prophets, followed by a commentary. The assembly then shared the great "benedictions," the first of which ended with the *kedushah* chant from Isaiah 6:3 — *"Holy, holy, holy is the Lord of hosts! All the earth is filled with his glory!"*

As long as the Christians were allowed in the synagogues, they took part in this biblical liturgy. After they were barred from the synagogues, they considered these biblical readings so basic that they added them to their domestic liturgies.

To these readings from the Old Testament new readings were gradually added — testimonies about Jesus in whom the Jewish Scriptures find their completion.

The commentary on the readings eventually became what is now the homily.

And, in time, the "Holy, holy, holy" found its place in the sequence, echoing the great events of the Covenant recalled by Scripture.

The Structure of the Mass: the Eucharistic Prayer

Why do we call the memorial of the bread and wine — the Body and Blood of Christ — the "Eucharistic Prayer"? When Jesus said "This is my body, this is my blood" on Holy Thursday evening, was he offering a prayer? The answer is yes. For at that supper Jesus celebrated the heart of the New Covenant, his Passover prayer of thanksgiving.

In line with Paul's insistence on a dignified and loving remembrance of the Last Supper, the early Christians instinctively inserted this precious remembrance into the ritual part of Jewish meals. This Jewish ritual included praise to the Most High. It also included a thanksgiving for the nourishment God gives in his Creation (the "grace" for the meal) and for the Covenant he has made with his People.

For Christians, the high point of the remembrance of God's gifts is the Eucharistic memorial of the New Covenant. (The word *eucharist* means "thanksgiving.")

The final element in the Jewish meal ritual was supplication for Israel. In the heart of the Eucharistic Prayer Christians, too, offer petition for "the Israel of God," the Church (Galatians 6:16).

The blending of this Christianized meal ritual with the liturgy of the Word from the synagogue took place with little trouble.

The Structure of the Mass: Sacrificial Communion

The Jewish Temple had a sacrificial liturgy which the synagogue did not have. Besides the Passover sacrifice of the Paschal lamb, other Temple sacrifices took place frequently. One of these sacrifices was the *Zebah Todah* (*Zebah* =

sacrifice; *Todah* = communion) in which a meal was shared with God.

Part of the *Zebah Todah* sacrifice was burnt up at the altar and part of it was given back to the offerer, who then ate it with friends. The sacrifice was also a meal.[2]

In the Bible certain meals are sacrifices. So anyone who considers the Mass a sacrifice and not a meal, or a meal and not a sacrifice, has lost touch with our Jewish roots. The Eucharistic Prayer is not just a blessing at a meal, it is a true sacrifice. It makes the meal a sacrifice whose source is the Jewish *Todah*.[3] This intimate bond between the "Mass" of the apostles and Jewish devotion is of far deeper consequence than our use of Jewish liturgical words like *Amen, Alleluia,* and *Hosanna*.

And finally, Jewish sacrifice-meals were repeated frequently, not celebrated only once a year. This fact gives us an insight into Jesus' intention regarding his memorial, the Christian Eucharist.

The Eucharistic Bread and Wine

Early Christian writings do not tell us what kind of bread and wine were used in the Eucharist. But Jewish custom of that period allows us to presume what Christian usage most likely was.

The bread used at the Jewish Passover meal had to be unleavened bread. But in Christian custom the bread used for consecration in the Eucharist was ordinarily chosen from the loaves brought by the faithful. This fact gives us reason to assume that it made no difference whether the bread used for consecration was leavened or unleavened.

It made no difference whether the wine used at the Passover meal was fermented wine or simply grape juice. This fact gives us reason to believe that it made no difference whether the wine used for consecration in the Eucharist was fermented wine or grape juice.

Christian Innovations

We have focused here on a number of things Christian liturgy has in common with its Jewish roots. But let us not forget that there are some basic differences between Jewish and Christian liturgies.[4]

For example, consider the Jewish and Christian liturgical feasts of Passover and Pentecost. They are identical in appearance but quite different in essence. Our Easter Passover no longer recalls only the great liberation from Egypt, it celebrates our liberation from death through the Resurrection of Jesus. And Pentecost no longer commemorates only the gift of the Law, the Ten Commandments, on Sinai. Our Christian Pentecost also celebrates God's gift to us of the inner law from the Spirit of Jesus.

Our liturgical week, with its final day of the Lord, is another thing that seems identical with Jewish practice. But the seventh day for Christians is not Saturday (the Sabbath) but Sunday, our weekly echo of Christ's passing over from death to New Life.

Also identical are the Psalms, which play an important role as meditation songs in the Eucharist. Indeed, the Law, the Prophets, and all of Israel's Scriptures are equally revered in Christian liturgy. But there is this difference: we interpret these Old Testament writings in the light of the Gospels and other New Testament writings. At Mass every passage we read from the Old Testament is understood with the consciousness of Jesus Christ.

Notes

1. See P. Benoit and M.-E. Boismard, *Synopse des quarte évangiles,* Les Editions du Cerf, Paris, II, 1972, page 381.
2. See Thomas J. Talley, "De la 'berakah' a l'eucharistie," *La Maison-Dieu* 125, 1976, page 28.
3. See P. Béguerie, *La Maison-Dieu* 125, 1976, page 44.

4. The author is very grateful to Rabbi S. Cohen, the private
   secretary of the Great Rabbinate of France. Rabbi Cohen
   graciously furnished invaluable information on Jewish liturgical customs in the time of the apostles.

2
The Mass in the
Time of the Persecutions
(A.D. 100 to A.D. 313)

A Time of Pain and Birth

The time of the persecutions was full of violent contrasts and conflicting facts. The few documents we possess from that period do not present a totally clear picture.

In those years the Church led a secret, clandestine life. Yet it was a life that was creative and colorful. Each local church community maintained its own traditions. But because of continuous contact — Christians traveling back and forth between East and West — the churches maintained communion with each other, and especially with the Church of Rome.

Bloody persecution was not the only threat to the Church. There were also vicious lies about Christians — for example, the claim that they practiced human sacrifice at their liturgies. And within the Church itself, there were harrowing controversies over liturgical matters which threatened to split the Church apart.

And yet, this was a key period in the history of the Mass. This time of persecutions was a dark night that gave birth, in the fourth and fifth centuries, to the dawn of a liturgical golden age.

But that was not all it gave birth to. In our own century the liturgical renewal of Vatican II sought its inspiration and framework in the rich experience of earlier tradition. Which period in liturgical history proved to be best suited to the needs of our time? None other than the time of the persecutions.

There are, finally, enlightening parallels between that time and ours. The confusion and conflict resulting from our Vatican II liturgical renewal are a bit like a replay of what took place during the reform at the start of the third century A.D.

The *Didache*: Preparatory Prayers for Eucharist

One of the earliest documents from the period of persecutions is called the *Didache* (pronounced DID-ah-kay). The word means, simply, the Doctrine or Instruction. Historians had known about this document, but they possessed no copies of it until after 1873 when it was discovered in Constantinople.

The *Didache* seems to have been a manual for missionaries who instructed rural Christian communities in Palestine and Syria. Most scholars date its composition anywhere from A.D. 100 to 150, or even as late as 180. Some, however, believe it is a much earlier text from the time of Saint Paul, with close ties to Jewish liturgy.

Scholars once thought that the *Didache* was a "how-to" manual for the Mass, because the author refers in several places to "eucharist" and "giving thanks." The frequent references to "eucharist" make the *Didache* look like a first-hand account of how the early Christians celebrated Mass. But that appearance is deceiving. The *Didache* seems, rather, to give Jewish-inspired prayers that are said at a Christian *agape* meal that *led up to* the Eucharist. These *agapes* and blessing prayers were for baptized Christians only, because they culminated in "the bread and wine of eternal life." In other words, the *Didache* seems to present a prayerful preparation for what we today call "Mass in the home."

The Prayers of the *Didache*

Jewish meals began with "the cup of blessing." To Jesus at the Last Supper, this cup symbolized God's coming kingdom or reign (read Luke 22:17-18). The *Didache* suggests the following prayer over this first cup:

We thank thee, our Father, for the holy vine of David
Thy servant, which Thou madest known to us through

Jesus Thy Servant; to Thee be the glory for ever.

These prayers at the beginning of the meal end with:

Even as this broken bread was scattered over the hills, and was gathered together and became one, so let Thy Church be gathered together from the ends of the earth into Thy kingdom; for Thine is the glory and the power through Jesus Christ for ever.

After the *agape* meal, the *Didache* leads into the Eucharistic mystery itself with the following prayer of thanks:

But after ye are filled, thus give thanks: We thank Thee, holy Father, for Thy holy name which Thou didst cause to tabernacle in our hearts, and for the knowledge and faith and immortality, which Thou madest known to us through Jesus Thy Servant; to Thee be the glory for ever.

The prayers after the *agape* include a "memento" for the Church (which our first Eucharistic Prayer places before the consecration — the memento for the living):

Remember, Lord, Thy Church, to deliver it from all evil and to make it perfect in Thy love, and gather it from the four winds, sanctified for Thy kingdom which Thou hast prepared for it; for Thine is the power and the glory for ever.

But then, at the point when the meal guests are about to receive the spiritual food and drink, the word-for-word prayers come to an abrupt halt. Here the *Didache* says only:

But permit the prophets to make Thanksgiving as much as they desire.

Why this silence about Jesus' words over the bread and wine?

The likely cause is the "discipline of the secret," an early Church practice of keeping the liturgical mysteries secret from those who were not initiated, that is, not baptized. The Gospel of John, written around the time of the *Didache*, is equally silent about Jesus' words over the bread and wine, despite the fact that Eucharistic symbolism abounds in John (read chapters 13 through 17 of John's Gospel).

As a recent study of the *Didache* points out: "Descriptions of the Eucharistic liturgy are infrequent in ancient Christian literature. That liturgy was considered an initiation rite whose ineffable character constituted the very essence of Christianity, and revelation of the mystery to the profane was to be avoided."[1]

Saint Clement of Rome's Letter to Corinth

Pope Clement of Rome wrote to the vibrant and turbulent Christians of Corinth around the years A.D. 95-98. Pope Clement did not go into detail about the liturgy of the Mass. What he did was to define a basic condition of its worthy celebration: unity around the bishop and his priests. In those days, as in the earlier days of Paul when some people declared themselves followers of Cephas and others followers of Apollos, Christianity in Corinth was again divided. Clement recalls it: "Even as far back as then you were forming cliques."

He continues:

It is disgraceful, beloved, yea, highly disgraceful, and unworthy of your Christian profession, that such a thing should be heard of as that the most stedfast and ancient Church of the Corinthians should, on account of one or two persons, engage in sedition against its presbyters (chapter 47).

Elsewhere Clement says:

We are of opinion, therefore, that those appointed by them, or afterwards by other eminent men, with the consent of the whole Church, and who have blamelessly served the flock of Christ in a humble, peaceable, and disinterested spirit, and have for a long time possessed the good opinion of all, cannot be justly dismissed from the ministry (chapter 44).

This unity around the ministers, Clement states, will manifest itself especially in liturgical celebration:

He (the Lord) has enjoined offerings (to be pre-

sented) and service to be performed (to Him), and that not thoughtlessly or irregularly, but at the appointed times and hours. . . . For his own peculiar services are assigned to the high priest, and their own proper place is prescribed to the priests, and their own special ministrations devolve on the Levites. The layman is bound by the laws that pertain to laymen (chapter 40).

So as early as the end of the first century, the successor of Peter was conscious of his authority in the Church, particularly in regard to the Eucharistic liturgy. Clement stressed very firmly that it was the role of the bishop and those priests who merited his confidence to preside over the celebration. Note the parallel between those ancient times and our own.

Saint Ignatius, Martyr

Ignatius, the bishop of Antioch who was martyred in the year 107, returns several times in his letters to the same subject Pope Clement emphasized: the unity of the people around their bishop and priests.

To the Christians of Ephesus, Saint Ignatius wrote:

Take heed, then, often to come together to give thanks to God, and show forth His praise (chapter 13).

To the Magnesians he wrote:

I exhort you to study to do all things with a divine harmony, while your bishop presides in the place of God, and your presbyters in the place of the assembly of the apostles, along with your deacons, who are most dear to me....Do ye therefore all run together as into one temple of God, as to one altar, as to one Jesus Christ . . . (chapters 6 and 7).

And to the Christians in Smyrna he wrote:

Let no man do anything connected with the Church without the bishop. Let that be deemed a proper Eucharist, which is (administered) either by the bishop, or by one to whom he has entrusted it (chapter 8).

The *First Apology* of Saint Justin, Martyr (*circa* A.D. 150)

Saint Justin was born in Syria. As a pagan philosopher he traveled widely in search of wisdom. He found that wisdom in Christianity. As a layman, Justin taught this highest wisdom in Rome and died a martyr between the years 163 and 167. Before he died, he wrote to the Emperor Antoninus Pius, and to his son, the future emperor and sage, Marcus Aurelius, in defense of Christianity. Christians are not godless, Justin wrote. On the contrary, they praise the true God. They celebrate a true sacrifice, but it is not a human sacrifice.

In his *First Apology,* Justin's first reference to the Mass goes as follows:

Having ended the prayers, we salute one another with a kiss. There is then brought to the president of the brethren bread and a cup of wine mixed with water; and he taking them gives praise and glory to the Father of the universe, through the name of the Son and of the Holy Ghost, and offers thanks at considerable length for our being counted worthy to receive these things at His hands (65).

Justin speaks of the Eucharist a second time, describing the Mass as it was celebrated in the second century A.D. Justin's description shows the essential elements of the Mass in the following centuries, and even of the Mass as it is celebrated today. He wrote:

And on the day called Sunday, all who live in cities or in the country gather together to one place, and the memoirs of the apostles or the writings of the prophets are read, as long as time permits; then, when the reader has ceased, the president verbally instructs, and exhorts to the imitation of these good things. Then we all rise together and pray, and, as we before said, when our prayer is ended, bread and wine and water are brought, and the president in like manner offers prayers and thanksgivings, according to his ability, and the people assent, saying Amen; and there is a distribution to each, and a participation of that over which thanks have been given, and to those who are absent a portion is sent by the deacons. And they who are well to do, and willing, give what each thinks fit; and what is collected is deposited with the president, who succours the orphans and widows, and those who, through sickness or any other cause are in want . . . (67).

In the above passage, Justin mentions several interesting facts.

• He clearly shows the two principal parts of the Mass: the liturgy of the Word and the Eucharistic liturgy. The liturgy of the Word concludes with what we today call the Prayer of the Faithful.

• He mentions no specific prayer by the celebrant when the offerings are brought. The Offertory or Preparation of the Gifts seems to flow right into the Eucharistic Prayer itself.

• The participation of the faithful in this Eucharistic Prayer seems to be restricted to the acclamation, "Amen!" (Other witnesses, writing slightly later than Justin, note that communicants approach the altar, and that lay persons or priests receive the consecrated bread in their hands.)

• The collection is not forgotten. Its purpose seems to have been a sharing of goods between the rich and the poor.

The Easter Controversy

This period in history gave rise to one of the saddest disputes that ever afflicted the Church: the controversy over the date of Easter. This conflict pitted great saints and genuine martyrs against each other. It was a conflict that touched the Eucharist directly because the Mass is the memorial of Christ's death and Resurrection.

In those days, as today, Easter was the great Christian feast of the year. But not all Christians celebrated it on the same date. Asiatic Christians observed it on the fourteenth day in the month of Nisan, the spring month in the Jewish calendar. So, for them, Easter could fall on a Tuesday, a Thursday, or even a Friday. To justify their custom, the Asiatics invoked the tradition of the apostles John and Philip.

Western Christians, meanwhile, started from a different principle: Christ rose on a Sunday, therefore Easter must be celebrated on a Sunday. The Western Christians took their stand on a tradition that came down from saints Peter and Paul. To complicate matters, Western Christians tended to suspect Asiatics of being in connivance with the Jews, which did not sit well.

Saint Polycarp, the Bishop of Smyrna in the East, came to Rome to defend the Asiatic stand. He conferred at length with Saint Anicetus, who was pope from 157 to 168. Their discussions settled nothing, but they separated good friends, and both eventually died martyrs.

The problem produced some scandalous situations. In Rome, for instance, Asiatics would celebrate the Resurrection in triumphant joy at the very time the Romans were reliving the sufferings of Holy Week. Tension reached such a level that, in some years, street fights broke out.

Exasperated by this ongoing scandal, Pope Victor convoked a council of the Asiatics in the year 191. When the council declared itself unanimously in favor of local Eastern tradition, the Pope reacted by threatening to excommunicate the Asiatics.

Fearful of a major split in the Church, Saint Irenaeus, the bishop of Lyons in Gaul, intervened. Asian-born, Irenaeus of Lyons followed Western customs while retaining a fond familiarity with Eastern ones. He was highly respected and loved in both East and West. In a letter to Pope Victor, Irenaeus recalled the example of Bishop Polycarp and Pope Anicetus when they had dealt with the same matter thirty years earlier. "Though adhering to different customs," Irenaeus wrote, "these two great men remained united, and they separated in peace."

In the days of old, Saint Peter had given in to the just views of Saint Paul (read Galatians 2:11-14). And now Peter's successor took the advice offered by the aged bishop of the Gauls. There was no more talk of excommunication and, little by little, the churches of Asia gradually adopted the Roman date for Easter.

Hippolytus of Rome
(The Beginning of the Third Century)

Hippolytus was a Roman priest who was perhaps born in Alexandria, and was perhaps also a bishop. (In the case of Hippolytus, "perhapses" abound!) His cultural background was Greek, and he wrote in Greek. He was a Scripture scholar and a theologian as well as a liturgist.

Hippolytus had violent doctrinal and personal clashes with two popes, Zephyrinus and Callistus. When Callistus became pope, Hippolytus broke away and, about the year 222, became history's first antipope. One motive Hippolytus may have had for the break was disappointment when he himself was not elected pope. His most evident motive was his bristling opposition to the introduction of Latin in the Roman liturgy in place of Greek.

Despite his "schism," Hippolytus and his writings are important. His most valuable written work is the *Apostolic Tradition*, composed around the year 215. The original Greek manuscript has never been found, but scholars possess translations of it in Coptic, Arabic, Ethiopian, and — ironically — in Latin.

For the occasion of the consecration of a bishop, the *Apostolic Tradition* presents a Eucharistic Prayer in the Roman tradition — the first detailed Eucharistic Prayer we possess. Compare this Eucharistic Prayer from Hippolytus with the second Eucharistic Prayer in our present-day missal and you cannot fail to see the connection: Pope Paul VI's source was, almost word for word, the ultraconservative Hippolytus.

The Eucharistic Prayer of Hippolytus

The new bishop lays his hand on the oblation and, "with all the presbyters" (this is a concelebrated Mass), gives thanks, saying:

The Lord be with you.
And the people shall say:
And with thy spirit.
Lift up your hearts.
We have them with the Lord.
Let us give thanks unto the Lord.
That is meet and right.

Then the bishop continues:

We render thanks unto thee, O God, through Thy Beloved Child Jesus Christ, Whom in the last times Thou didst send to us to be a Savior and Redeemer and the Messenger of Thy counsel;

Who is Thy Word inseparable from Thee, through Whom Thou madest all things and in Whom Thou wast well-pleased;

Whom Thou didst send from heaven into the Virgin's womb and Who conceived within her was made flesh and demonstrated to be Thy Son being born of Holy Spirit and a Virgin;

Who fulfilling Thy will and preparing for Thee a holy people stretched forth His hands for suffering that He might release from sufferings them who have believed in Thee;

(Some ancient versions of the *Apostolic Tradition* introduced the *Sanctus* at this point, which was not provided by Hippolytus).

Who when He was betrayed to voluntary suffering that He might abolish death and rend the bonds of the devil and tread down hell and enlighten the righteous and establish the ordinance and demonstrate the resurrection:

Taking bread and making eucharist (i.e., giving thanks) to Thee said: Take eat: this is My Body which is broken for you (for the remission of sins). Likewise also the cup, saying: This is My Blood which is shed for you.

When ye do this (ye) do My "anamnesis" (remembrance).

Doing therefore the "anamnesis" of His death and resurrection we offer to Thee the bread and cup making eucharist to Thee because Thou has bidden us (or, found us worthy) to stand before Thee and minister as priests to Thee.

And we pray Thee that (Thou wouldest send Thy Holy Spirit upon the oblation of Thy holy Church) Thou wouldest grant to all Thy Saints who partake to be united (to Thee) that they may be fulfilled with the Holy Spirit for the confirmation of their faith in truth,

that we may praise and glorify Thee through Thy (Beloved) Child Jesus Christ through whom glory and honor be unto Thee with the Holy Spirit in Thy holy Church now and for ever and world without end. Amen.

Latin As the Language of the Liturgy

All of the New Testament writings were composed in Greek, and when they were read aloud at liturgical gatherings they were read in Greek.

The first apostles of Rome were Greeks or people who expressed themselves in Greek. In the early years of Christianity, even in Rome, the language of literature and culture was Greek. In the middle of the second century, for example, the Emperor Marcus Aurelius, a Roman, wrote his famous *Meditations* in Greek.

Latin, meanwhile, was dismissed as a "vulgar" language. For over three centuries the only place where Christian writers made Latin their chosen medium of expression was North Africa.[2]

But in Rome there was a large group of people who spoke nothing but Latin — the common people. And it so happened that from A.D. 217 to 222, Rome had a very capable pope who had been born a slave — Pope Saint Callistus. By this time Christianity had its intellectuals and aristocrats. But Pope Callistus felt close to the many ordinary people who understood no Greek. So this pope decided that, in Rome at least, Latin should be the language of the liturgy.

The introduction of Latin into the liturgy turned things topsy-turvy. Greek-speaking Christians reacted violently, and there is good reason to think that the fiery Hippolytus led the opposition, denouncing the change as "demagoguery."

Nevertheless, the enforced changeover was far from abrupt; the Roman liturgy was not completely Latinized until the second half of the fourth century, about 150 years after Hippolytus opposed the change. And then in the seventh century, when Greek Christians again became very numerous in Rome, the liturgy returned to being bilingual, mingling prayers in Latin and Greek. Even today, at the papal Mass in Saint Peter's Basilica in Rome, the Epistle and Gospel are read both in Latin and in Greek, reflecting traces of that era.

Liturgical Creativity

During this epoch and into the fourth century, improvisation in liturgy was the rule rather than the exception. This was especially true regarding the prayers of the Mass. There was no "apostolic liturgy" from which all later ones would derive. Ancient documents show that celebrants of the Eucharist were free, within limits, to compose their own prayers and organize the ritual.

This practice, of course, involved some risk of deviation from tradition; not every priest or bishop was a brilliant theologian. As a rule, however, the leader of a community was a trustworthy man, carefully chosen from a solid Christian background. And the people he led were quite sensitive in matters of fidelity to tradition. Liturgical improvisation did not open the door to celebrants doing or saying anything they pleased.

Mass prayers that became known for their excellence were copied and then used in other Christian communities. One of the Eucharistic Prayers in circulation was the one Hippolytus presented in his *Apostolic Tradition*. That he was not the only one to circulate his prayers is shown by the fact that other texts were preferred to his.

Other Features of the Liturgy

There are a few more features of the liturgy in this period that deserve at least brief attention because, in centuries that followed, these same features would become the focus of problems to which the period of persecutions provides precedent solutions. Here is a brief list.

The celebrant's vestments. During this period of history no special vestments were worn, though it was understood that the celebrant would wear the best clothing he possessed.

The place of the celebrant. Where the celebrant sat or stood depended on circumstances. When the Mass was celebrated in connection with a meal, the priest naturally sat at the table with the others, just as Jesus did at the Last Supper.

When the Mass was celebrated in a private home, the celebrant stood near the table, surrounded by the faithful — the *circumstantes* or bystanders — as some ancient texts point out.

When the Mass was celebrated in a catacomb on the tomb of a martyr, the celebrant had his back to the people because these tombs were hollowed out of walls.

As regards the location of the people, men and women were separated in some communities — a policy which Hippolytus calls for in his *Apostolic Tradition*, in connection with the kiss of peace. The kiss of peace had long since fallen into disuse in most places. But the custom of separating men and women continued in some regions, a practice many liturgical scholars trace back to the kiss of peace.[3]

Holy Communion. The bread and wine to be consecrated at Mass were taken from the offerings people brought for distribution among the poor. It was ordinary bread and wine, prepared in no special way.

People received Communion standing. They took the consecrated bread in their hands and drank the consecrated wine from the chalice. Then, if they wished, they carried away consecrated bread to give to others who were absent, or to receive themselves during the following week. In the *Apostolic Tradition* Hippolytus recommends that they watch over this consecrated bread with care.

The pope would send Eucharistic bread to priests who were going to celebrate Mass in other parishes in Rome, and to bishops to whom he wished to show his friendship and unity in Christ. A small amount of consecrated bread was also reserved for the next day's Mass. At that Mass it was placed in the chalice which had just been consecrated, to symbolize the unity of all Masses in the one sacrifice of Christ.

Concluding Observations

This period in liturgical history — A.D. 100 to 313 — saw two major conflicts: the Easter controversy and the schism of Hippolytus. Neither conflict brought about a split in the Church.

The Easter controversy took place between the Asiatics and the Romans, the East and the West. Saint Polycarp represented the Eastern tradition and Pope Anicetus upheld the West. When the controversy flared up a generation later, Saint Irenaeus urged Pope Victor to show moderation. The solution of the controversy was a form of pluralism; the opposing customs regarding the date of Easter did not constitute a rupture in the unity of faith, and so both customs were allowed in the interest of peace.

In the second conflict, Pope Callistus wanted Latin in the liturgy for the good of the common folk. In opposition, Hippolytus fought to conserve Greek against the innovation of Latin. Hippolytus represented "the conservative tendency"; he saw the abandonment of Greek as merely the tip of an iceberg — a symptom of growing laxity in faith and morals.

The schism was shortlived. Ten years after his break, Hippolytus and a new pope, Pontianus, were both exiled in Sardinia. Pontianus succeeded in getting Hippolytus to renounce his title of antipope and to call his followers back to the fold. The schism ended in reconciliation, and Hippolytus died a martyr in A.D. 235.

The Latin and Greek languages existed side by side in the liturgy for over a century. A pluralism in which each person could pray "in his own tongue" (Acts 2:11) was enjoyed by the very people who opposed such pluralism. In the fourth century, Latin gained ascendency in the liturgy, but only because by that time fewer people in society spoke Greek.

The history of the Mass during the years of persecution is a story of creativity and conflict. The story suggests lessons for our time — lessons of dialogue, patience, and hope.

Notes

1. See *La doctrine des douze apôtres (Didaché), introduction, texte, traduction par Willy Rordorf and André Tuilier, coll. "Sources chrétiennes,"* no. 248, Les Editions du Cerf 1978, page 40.
2. Pierre de Labriolle, *Histoire de la littérature latine chrétienne,* Edition *"Les Belles Lettres,"* Paris 1924, page 79.
3. A.-G. Martimort, ed. *The Church at Prayer: Introduction to the Liturgy,* page 98 (Desclée Company, New York).

3
The Golden Age
of the Eucharistic Liturgy
(A.D. 313 to A.D. 604 —
The 4th, 5th, and 6th Centuries)

"The Golden Age" is the title given to the liturgical epoch that spanned the Peace of Constantine in A.D. 313 and the death of Saint Gregory the Great in 604. The title is appropriate. And yet, in both the civil and the religious spheres, things were far from perfect during this period.

Invasions, Heresies, and Liturgy

This was the age of the barbarian invasions. Routed by the Chinese in Mongolia, the Huns moved westward and bore down on the Slavs. Moving around in the vast plains they inhabited, the Slavs kept out of harm's way as the torrent passed through. The hordes thundered onward, threatening the Roman Empire in both the East and the West.

The East suffered so heavily that Constantinople, the new capital of the empire, was forced to negotiate. In the West, the Huns pushed through Germany and on to Orleans before they were stopped in battle at the Catalaunian Plains in A.D. 451. There was devastation everywhere.

The destruction was all the more terrible because other tribes, fleeing before the Huns, pillaged as they went. The Vandals crossed Gaul and Spain, sacking the cities in their path. They then turned southward and invaded North Africa, one of the most beautiful provinces of the empire and of Christianity. During his last agony, Saint Augustine knew that the barbarian hordes were laying siege to his episcopal city, Hippo, in North Africa. The future appeared so bleak to Augustine that he died believing this was the end of the world. It was the year 430.

Nor was the rest of Europe spared. The Angles crossed the

Channel, pushed back the Celts, and took root in England which now bears their name.

In 406, Rome was pillaged by Alaric and the Visigoths. Fifty-six years later, in 462, Attila the Hun advanced to the very gates of Rome, and it took the courage and prestige of Pope Saint Leo to save the city. Ninety years later, in 552, Rome narrowly avoided destruction from the Ostrogoths. But on their heels the terrible Longbeards — the Lombards — rose up. Twice Pope Gregory the Great negotiated, begging the barbarians to spare Rome — first in 598, and again in 604 on the eve of his death.

After the invasions subsided, barbarian invaders remained in Europe and were absorbed into the population. One of the Church's tasks now was to bring the Gospel to them — and to fashion a liturgy suited to their culture.

No less dramatic was the situation in Christianity. The schism of Donatus (which began around the year 312) drenched the Church of Africa with blood, and then poisoned Italy.

In the Near East, meanwhile — during the first quarter of the fourth century — Arianism triggered still another disastrous schism which struck at the very roots of the liturgy by denying the divinity of Christ. Arianism swept across the entire Mideast and filtered into Italy. When the Goths penetrated into Gaul, they brought the rampant virus of heresy with them. As Saint Jerome exclaimed, "The whole world woke up Arian."

Wave after wave of invasion — the breakdown of basic social order — radical insecurity of life and property — famines and epidemics: these were the circumstances in which the liturgy, against all odds, expanded and diversified and gained stability.

Exceptional Church Leaders in East and West

In a sense, the odds were even. For during these times the Lord gave his Church outstanding bishops. In the East there were legendary leaders such as saints Basil, John Chrysostom, Ephrem, Cyril of Alexandria, and Cyril of Jerusalem. And in the West there were saints Ambrose, Augustine, Leo the Great, and Gregory the Great. These men are called "Fathers of the Church." They deserve the title not only because they were great "doctors (teachers) of the faith" but also because they were "Fathers of the liturgy." They brought liturgy to such a state of beauty and maturity that what we have today, in its essential features, is what they gave us. The Byzantine liturgy we owe to Saint John Chrysostom. The Milanese liturgy we inherited from Saint Ambrose. And for the Roman liturgy we can thank Saint Gregory the Great.

One of the great merits of these master liturgists was the sensitivity they had for the needs and tastes of their people. The liturgy they developed so mirrored the Christian people's relationship to God that people clung to it as a deep expression of their lives. There is an insight here that is just as valid today as when it was grasped fifteen centuries ago.

Church Buildings and Wealth

To appreciate the creative activity of this period, one need only look at what is most visible. According to the evidence gathered by Josef Jungmann,[1] even before the end of the persecutions there were more than forty churches in the city of Rome alone.

Following the example set by his pagan predecessors, the Emperor Constantine gave the Christian Church numerous buildings for worship. Some of these buildings were so magnificent that they were called "royal" — in Greek, *basilicoi*.

To maintain these basilicas, the empire allocated funds that were just as royal. The people had very little; many of them lived in poor if not wretched conditions. The empire owned practically everything and possessed untold wealth. But at least the resources that went for worship made it possible for the Church to relieve some of the misery.

The Clothing Worn for Liturgy

In the earliest centuries, everyday clothing was worn at liturgical celebrations. Those who conducted worship often went to the liturgy right after work, or took time off from work. In Rome, up to about the year 428, there were no special vestments or insignia for priests and others who performed liturgical functions. Quite the opposite, in fact. In the fifth century, Pope Celestine I (A.D. 422 to 432) wrote the following words of correction to the bishops of Vienne and Narbonne in Gaul:

We must distinguish ourselves from the people by doctrine, not by vestment; by manners, not by habit; by purity of spirit, not by adornment....We must instruct and not deceive. It is not a matter of inspiring the eyes, but of teaching souls.[2]

Liturgical celebrants and other ministers wore regular clothing of good quality. In Rome, this meant a robe of white linen — the *tunica* — and another vestment over it. Little by little, however, a new custom caught on. Celebrants continued to wear the same type of clothing, but the particular garments they wore to worship were not worn at other times. They were beautiful clothes cut from finer cloth. Eventually these clothes acquired so many special trimmings that they were known as liturgical "ornaments." Finally, after the type of clothing people wore became entirely different, these same vestments continued to be worn in the liturgy — silent witnesses of a bygone era.

Liturgical Ceremonies and Music

The early Christians met in small family groups for "the breaking of the bread." As Christians became more numerous, so did the groups. When the persecutions ended and Christianity became the privileged religion of the empire under Constantine, the groups became crowds. Now there was need for attention to order and precision.

The Romans had a particularly keen sense of order. It did

not take them long to decide the exact roles played by celebrant and faithful. For many years the precise order of celebration was passed down from one master of ceremonies to the next by word of mouth and practice. Then the order of ceremonies was gradually put in writing. The first of these documents — the Roman *ordos* — were drawn up at the request of Frankish churches who wanted to know how the ceremonies were done in Rome.

In Milan, Saint Ambrose (c. 340-397) favored the chanting of hymns by the people. Ambrose wrote several hymns which have survived.

The form of liturgical singing known as Gregorian chant characterized the Latin liturgy for a thousand years. The earliest of the so-called Gregorian melodies date from the seventh century. There is no documentation to show how directly these compositions are attributable to Pope Gregory the Great (c. 540-604). But the fact that they were named after Gregory lends weight to the view that his reform of the Mass prayers included a definite interest in the singing at Mass.

During this period liturgical music was exclusively vocal; musical instruments were still considered too tainted with paganism to be used in church. And during this period all of the chant was monody or one-part singing. Religious polyphony did not arrive on the scene until the Middle Ages.

The Texts Used in the Liturgy

During this period liturgical prayers, especially the prayers of the Mass, tended to be put in writing. Bishops retained the right to improvise their own prayers, but from the end of the fourth century written compositions were recommended. Bishops gradually composed liturgical booklets for their personal use.

Now that these booklets existed, Saint Augustine complained that some bishops were using not only mediocre texts, but texts composed by heretics and full of their errors.

In the West some bishops did not compose original prayer

formulas. Instead, they adopted prayer formulas copied from the Lateran archives where the *libelli* — the "little books" — of famous popes were kept in collections. The texts used by bishops were not like the complete missals in use before the Second Vatican Council. They were hand-copied booklets, divided according to function. There was one for the celebrant, one for the lector, and one for the cantor.

On the Sacraments, a work attributed to Saint Ambrose of Milan ,[3] cites a Eucharistic Prayer that coincides almost word for word with the Roman Canon (what has become our Eucharistic Prayer I). It says:

And the priest says:

Remembering, therefore, his very glorious passion and resurrection from the underworld and his ascension into heaven, we offer thee this spotless host, this spiritual host, this unbloody host, this sacred bread and this chalice of eternal life.

And we beseech and pray thee to accept this offering on thy celestial altar through the hands of angels.

As it pleased thee to accept the gifts of Abel the Just One, the sacrifice of our father Abraham and that which thy high priest Melchisedech offered thee. (4,27)

Ambrose also explains: "When thou beggest (communion), the priest says to thee: 'the body of Christ' and thou repliest: 'Amen,' that is to say: 'that is true.' What thy tongue confesseth, may thy heart ratify." (25)

So, in asking communicants to respond "Amen" when they receive the Body and Blood, Pope Paul VI restored a very ancient rite.

Diversification and Eastern Liturgies

As it continued to develop and stabilize, the liturgy also diversified. This had already been going on unnoticed before Constantine, when the Church was living in semi-concealment. After the Peace of Constantine it came to the surface and spread without restraint.

For various reasons there came to be a wider and wider distinction between Eastern and Western liturgies. This divergence was heightened by Constantine's move from Rome to Constantinople. The empire now had two capitals: the civil one in the East and the religious one in the West. As life went on, diversification proceeded without plan or program and at the mercy of circumstances.

In the East diversification was totally spontaneous. In this part of the empire there was no central religious authority. The bishops of the new capital, Constantinople, tried to gain that authority. But the well-established patriarchs of Antioch, Alexandria, and Jerusalem took a dim view of encroachments on their liberty and the unique character of their liturgies.

Over the course of centuries the following liturgies developed in the East:

1. A Greek liturgy began in Antioch, which was then the capital of Syria. Like Jerusalem, with which it was closely linked, the patriarchate of Antioch had been founded by saints Peter and Paul. This liturgy spread to Byzantium and became known as *Byzantine*. Saint John Chrysostom, born in Antioch and named patriarch of Constantinople in A.D. 398, probably brought the liturgy of Antioch with him to Constantinople (Byzantium). The Byzantine rite was later named the Liturgy of Saint John Chrysostom.

The same Greek liturgy of Antioch influenced the *Armenian* rites, then the *Georgian,* and later the *Ukrainian* (or Ruthenian) rites.

2. Antioch also developed a *Syriac* liturgy, of which the *Maronite* rite practiced in Libya is a variant. The Maronite rite gave birth to the *Chaldean* rite to the East, and to the *Malabar* rite in far-off India.

3. In Egypt, the great city of Alexandria celebrated its liturgies in Greek for a long time. Welcoming Roman and Syrian influences, it created the *Coptic* and *Ethiopian* liturgies in the languages of those countries of Africa.

So in the East at this time we find ten languages, ten different liturgies, but one and the same Eucharist.

Liturgies of the West

Diversification was evident also in the West. There were two main branches.

The first was the Italo-African branch which — besides the Roman liturgy — included the *Milanese* or Ambrosian rite, and the one Augustine celebrated in *Africa*.

The second was the Ibero-Gallican branch which had Byzantine influences. This branch comprised:
- the *Gallican* liturgy, celebrated in Gaul;
- the *Gothic* liturgy, known later in Spain as the Mozarabic liturgy;
- the *Celtic* liturgy in Britain and Ireland.

Rather than speak of liturgies, it would be more exact to speak of liturgical "families." All of these liturgies had local variations. Jungmann tells of "innumerable local varieties in relation to the custom of parcelling out in that epoch."

In the West, the populations reached by the Gospel were descendants of the barbarian invaders. These populations were just barely rooted, or in the process of taking root. Ethnic groups had only a rudimentary culture and no written language. For a long time the language used in dealings with Roman administrators was Latin. Latin was also the most convenient means of communication between small tribes which spoke different dialects — Gallic, Celtic, Frankish, Burgundian, and Gothic. Already the maxim held true: "Wine and Latin go everywhere." So, why go to the trouble of translating the Mass into Gallic or Gothic or Frankish dialects? In Gaul as in Rome, the liturgy passed quite naturally from Greek to Latin.

The Reform of Pope Saint Gregory

The Roman Mass was developing under the guidance of remarkable popes such as saints Leo the Great (A.D. 440 to

461) and Gelasius (A.D. 492 to 496). And at the best possible time, to sum up and complete the development, the Lord gave his Church a pope of even greater significance: Saint Gregory the Great — the only pope, along with Saint Leo, to merit the title "Great."

Born into a family of Roman patricians, Gregory was Roman through and through. A specialist in Roman law, he functioned at high levels in Roman administration and even became prefect of Rome. Gregory was no stranger to the workings of the world when he renounced human concerns to become a monk. He now entered a new area of expertise — the spiritual school of another distinguished Roman, Saint Benedict. Some time later, the pope took Gregory from his monastery and made him the papal representative to Constantinople, where he became familiar with Eastern diplomacy and liturgy. Finally, in the year 590, he was elected pope. In the midst of papal preoccupations, Gregory never forgot this guideline from the Rule of his spiritual father, Saint Benedict: "Let nothing...be put before the Work of God" — the praise of God in sacred liturgy.

Pope Gelasius had already gathered the prayers of the Eucharistic liturgy into three books: a *temporal* (for feasts such as Christmas, Easter, and Pentecost), a *sanctoral* (for feasts of saints), and a book of *votive Masses* (for such and such an intention). Gregory condensed these three books into one, the forerunner of our missal. He made corrections and clarifications, all with Roman moderation. The result was a coherent, organized whole.

It would be claiming too much to say that Gregory's work escaped criticism. In one case, John, the bishop of Syracuse in Sicily, accused him of tampering with the "apostolic prayer." Gregory replied that John's attack was unjustified because there had never been an "apostolic prayer" to start with; he had had to make changes because the text formerly in use was so shoddy that it must have been composed by some mediocre scholar. Only a pope, and a pope of Gregory's stature, could afford such a remark.

Changes in Liturgical Terminology

Another significant factor in the evolution of Western liturgy during the Golden Age was the introduction of two liturgical terms.

The first term, the word *Canon,* came to stand for the central part of the Mass, what we today call "the Eucharistic Prayer." *Canon* means "rule." In connection with the Mass, it meant the prayer that the celebrant was obliged to say without changing anything in it. At the beginning of Christianity, the Eucharistic Prayer had been left to the initiative of the celebrant. But in Rome, from the time of Pope Innocent I (A.D. 401 to 417), it became one fixed formula "by rule." They ended up calling it "the rule" — the Canon.

The second term was the word *Mass.* In the early years of the Church, Christians spoke of the "breaking of bread," of the "great prayer," then of the "eucharist." But even before the time of Saint Gregory, another term was being used — the term *Mass.*[4]

The term *Canon* came down from Church authority. The term *Mass* — from the Latin *missa* — developed from use among the people. Unlike earlier names, the word *Mass* does not tell us anything about the Eucharistic mystery. All the word *missa* really means is "dismissal." (The ceremony is over; you are dismissed.) Yet this is the term that took hold and continued in use up until Vatican II when the term *Eucharist* regained some of its former standing. People today still speak of the "Mass" because the word continues to suggest the remembrance of Christ in the way Catholics have known it.

The Papal Mass in the Time of Gregory the Great

The Mass, as arranged by Pope Gregory, was a ceremony of great splendor. The Mass had come a long way from the more or less clandestine celebrations in homes and catacombs. Here is how Gregory's Mass unfolded.

The pope leaves the Lateran palace on horseback and rides

toward the basilica where Mass will be celebrated. He is accompanied by the entire pontifical court — priests, faithful, and a retinue of high officials. Besides being the religious head of a very large community, the pope has become the true master and fearless defender of Rome. (Recall that Pope Gregory negotiated with the Lombards for the survival of Rome in the year 592.) This fact accounts for the pontifical Mass being both a religious and civil event.

A party of priests from the chosen basilica welcomes the pope and his retinue on their arrival. Led to the sacristy, the pontiff dons vestments for the Mass. A cleric gives him the names of those who will read the Epistle and the Gospel, and that of the soloist for the principal chants. The choir and all the junior clerics are ready and waiting.

Before the pope's entrance, the rest of the clergy form a semicircle behind the altar, facing the people. In the middle of the semicircle is the chair reserved for the pope. Informed that everything is ready, the pope orders candles to be lit, and the chant of the *Introit* (an antiphon and psalm) to be intoned. The procession gets underway.

The pope makes his solemn entry into the church. As he nears the altar, he gives the kiss of peace to the bishop of the place and to the priests. He then kisses the altar and the book from which the Gospel will be read. He takes his place in the midst of the clergy and gives the signal for chanters to skip to the *Gloria Patri* which concludes the *Introit* psalm.

The pope celebrates Mass turned toward the East. In Rome, churches have their sanctuary in the West. The pope presides from the front of the church — turned toward the people.

Only the choir chants the *Kyrie eleison* (a carry-over from the Greeks, doubtless from the time of Pope Gelasius — A.D. 492 to 496), while the pope prays silently. On feast days the very ancient *Gloria in excelsis* is then sung. Afterward, there is the chanting of a prayer.

There are only two readings. Between readings a soloist

and the choir alternate a chant. The second reading, the Gospel, is done very solemnly.

Offertory preparations are long. As a psalm is chanted, clerics pass through the assembly collecting bread and wine brought by the faithful. People pour their little flasks of wine into chalices. Later in the Mass small amounts from the consecrated cup will be poured back into these chalices.

After these preparations the ministers wash their hands. The pope also washes his hands, having personally received the bread brought by the high Roman nobility. The pontiff then goes to the altar and signals to the choir to conclude their chant. Now there is silence as the pope prays quietly. He concludes in a loud voice: *"Per omnia saecula saeculorum."*

Next come the Preface, the *Sanctus,* and the Canon. The Canon and the words of consecration are recited in a low tone; only those nearby can hear the words distinctly. The consecrated bread and the chalice are not raised until the end of the Canon, at the *Per ipsum.* Gregory decreed that the *Pater noster* should follow immediately, with its supplement, the *Libera nos.*

Once more now the ministers are busy, dividing the bread and giving the kiss of peace to the people. The divided bread is put into little bags which are then distributed to the bishops and priests so that they can break the bread into smaller pieces. For Communion from the cup, the chalices containing the wine from the people are brought forward, and a bit of the precious Blood is poured into each chalice.

During the singing of the *Agnus Dei* (recently borrowed from the Eastern Church), the pope, sitting in his chair, signals to the court officials, inviting them to his table. The pope receives Communion. Immediately afterward, the archdeacon makes the announcements, and those who are not receiving Communion now leave. (This practice makes it easier to distribute Communion to those who remain. But at a future date some will find in it a justification for distributing Communion after Mass.)

Once Communion has ended, there is a concluding prayer at the altar. Then the dismissal is announced — *"Ite, missa est"* — without a last blessing. Finally there is the recessional.

Influence of the Roman Liturgy

This splendid Roman liturgy was still purely local, limited to the diocese of Rome. During the fifth, sixth, and even the seventh centuries it does not seem to have scaled the mountains to the north, nor to have crossed over Monte Cassino to the south. It was still used only within a few kilometers around Rome. As Dom Cabrol notes, "This local character is even more accentuated in the Roman liturgy than in other Western liturgies. Roman martyrs and saints, Roman usages, Roman events hold preponderant parts in it. Its calendar is likewise local, and will become universal only around the thirteenth century."[5]

In the third century, Firmilian of Caesarea came from the East to Rome, passing through many different provinces on route. He noted: "Not only in the celebration of Easter, but in many other points, the Romans have their own customs, quite different from those in Jerusalem. In most of the provinces, depending on the places and the people, many things are different without, for all that, any of them detaching themselves from the peace and the unity of the Catholic Church."[6] Far from being shocked by such diversity, people found it normal and welcomed it.

In the fifth century, right in the middle of the Golden Age, a scribe from Gaul made the long journey to Rome to see and copy down what they were doing there. He was impressed, and expressed his veneration for Roman liturgy. He even affirmed that his church "wishes to follow the example of Rome." However, he claimed for his church "some independence in the choice of its own customs."[7]

The very local character of the Roman liturgy accounted for its limited influence during the Golden Age. But by the end of this period, it was ready to spread to the rest of the Church in the West. It now contained:

— a central, fixed text: the Roman Canon;
— an established language: Latin;
— a well-adapted chant: plainsong;
— a ceremonial which had proven itself.

The Roman liturgy was a balanced, polished, time-tested whole which could be "exported" anywhere without needing anything added to it. And during centuries to come, other Western liturgies would feel the need to draw upon its resources.

Notes

1. Josef A. Jungmann, S.J., *The Mass of the Roman Rite*, Volume One, page 50, note 3.
2. Migne, *Patrologia Latina*, Volume 50, col. 431.
3. Saint Ambrose wrote a treatise on Baptism and Eucharist entitled *On the Mysteries* which does not cite any prayers of the Mass. At a series of homilies for catechumens given by Ambrose around the year 390, an auditor took notes. In these homilies Ambrose cited prayers of the Mass, which the auditor wrote down. What we have from the auditor — *On the Sacraments* — bears a clear resemblance to Ambrose's own *On the Mysteries*.
4. Jungmann, Volume One, pages 174-175.
5. Dom Cabrol, in *Liturgia, Encyclopédie populaires des connaissances liturgiques, éd, Blond et Gay,* Paris 1943, page 502.
6. Dom Cabrol, in *Liturgia,* Op. cit. page 375.
7. Dom Cabrol, in *Liturgia,* Op. cit. page 375.

PART TWO
The Mass in the Middle Ages
(A.D. 604 to A.D. 1517)

4 The Dialogue Between Rome and Gaul

5 Roman Tradition and the Carolingian Renaissance

6 The Gothic Mass

4
The Dialogue Between Rome and Gaul
(A.D. 604 to A.D. 751)

In the West, the Middle Ages were a time of give-and-take between papal Rome and the newly Christianized barbarian populations. In the process, the unifying influence of Rome sometimes predominated. But sometimes Rome ended up endorsing elements of Northern European piety. The result was change in the Eucharistic liturgy.

During the first phase — from the death of Gregory the Great in 604 to the accession of Pepin the Short, proclaimed King of the Franks in 751 — the dialogue was prepared, and the actors took their places. These were troubled centuries. Teeming vitality marked the barbarian peoples. Papal Rome, meanwhile, set an example as a model of order and unifying clarity. This Roman characteristic accounted for the interest in the Roman liturgical books called sacramentaries.

The Backwash of History

A frightful invasion again overran Gaul, this time from the south. The Saracens — Islamic invaders — crossed over the Pyrenees mountains from Spain and advanced to Poitiers. It was there that Charles Martel, "the Hammer of the Infidels," crushed them decisively. As threatening as it was to the West, that was the only invasion that took place during this period.

The civil and social situation was stabilizing. Below the Loire River in Gaul, there was mixed blood, a blend of the ancient Gallo-Roman with the Visigothic.

East and southeast of what would become France were the Goths. The stature of the Goths left Sidonius Apollinarius (A.D. 430 to 487) so awestruck that he called them "men seven feet tall." Sidonius had reason to say this; he had had to defend his episcopal city, Clermont-Ferrand, against them. The Goths finally banded together and settled down in Burgundy.

The Franks, meanwhile, already occupied the Ile-de-France, the northeast of Gaul, and a good part of what would become Belgium.

These tribes were like moving ethnic strata. They collided and fought to gain supremacy or independence. But these collisions did not change the state of affairs to any great degree. Much more precarious, at this time and for centuries to come, was the situation in Italy.

The Liturgies of Ancient Gaul

The ancient Gallo-Roman population was now decimated and became a fringe group. With its decline, Gallo-Roman culture faded away. There would be no more Roman civil servants of the stature of Ambrose or Gregory the Great. There were still some great bishops like Caesarius of Arles (A.D. 502 to 542), but these were no longer men steeped in the classical culture of Greece and Rome. They had other pre-occupations, mainly in the moral order. Following the intense creativity of the earlier liturgical periods, this era was one of assimilation.

Rather than "Gallican liturgies," it would be better to speak of the "liturgies of the Gauls," meaning all the Western non-Roman liturgies. (The African church of Saint Augustine had, unfortunately, withered away.)

The Milanese or Ambrosian liturgy. As far as the Romans were concerned, everything north of Rome was Gallic and barbarian — even Milan. Milanese liturgy, however, was still closely related to the Roman. Saint Ambrose declared that he was following Roman tradition, though he did adopt some liturgical practices from north of the Alps. The Ambrosian liturgy preserved elements from earlier centuries that Rome had abandoned. The Ambrosian Canon, for example, was a form of the primitive Roman Canon.

The Celtic liturgy was strongly influenced by a number of

powerful monasteries. This was the liturgy of the rugged Celtic apostles of Ireland — great Frankish and Saxon missionary voyagers like saints Columban and Boniface. This liturgy borrowed freely from liturgies on the Continent. The Celts were fiercely attached to their liturgy and it lasted for centuries before being forced out. In the year 818, King Louis the Pious imposed the Roman liturgy on French Brittany. And after the conquest of Ireland by the English, the English synod of Cashel in 1172 called upon all the churches of Ireland to adopt the Anglo-Roman rite.

The Visigoth or Spanish liturgy. Manuscripts from the tenth and eleventh centuries show that, before the Islamic occupation, the kingdom of the Visigoths had a rich and organized liturgy. This liturgy was different in origin from the Roman and was strongly influenced by Eastern rites. It had considerable impact on the liturgies of Gaul, the southwest of which formed part of the Visigoth kingdom. Popes tried repeatedly to replace it with the Roman liturgy, but no one succeeded until Pope Gregory VII gave the command in the eleventh century. Even then the Spanish liturgy did not disappear; Cardinal Ximenes obtained permission to preserve it in several churches in Toledo.

The Gallican liturgy properly so-called. The liturgy of ancient Gaul is less well known to us than the Visigothic because little of it survived the eighth-century reform of Charlemagne. The Gallican liturgy was closely related to its Spanish cousin; it too was influenced by Eastern rites, especially the Syrian. It included gestures and prayers from the primitive liturgy of Rome and other centers.

The Gallican Mass

Nevertheless, we know several original features in the Gallican Mass from the time of Caesarius of Arles (A.D. 502 to 542) as it was celebrated in the Provence region. It had these features in the sixth century and retained them up until the eighth-century reform of Pepin the Short and Charlemagne.[1]

One outstanding feature of the Mass was *processions,* which the Gallican people loved. Another feature was the number *three.* Whether it was written prayers or chants, everything seemed to come in *threes.* This was probably due to the doctrine of the Trinity, which the Church had defended against Arianism and its fifth-century offshoots. (Saint Hilary of Poitiers had vigorously defended the true doctrine in his masterpiece, *On the Trinity,* written in 356-360.) Later on, these *threes* might also have been in reaction to Islam and its denial of the Trinity.

The Gallican Mass went as follows:

The liturgy begins with an entrance procession of the clergy. The accompanying chant ends with the *"Gloria Patri et Filio et Spiritui Sancto."* (The Council of Vaison in 529 added *"sicut erat in principio"* — "as it was in the beginning" — to emphasize that the divinity of the Son is from all eternity. This region of Gaul, more than any other, was careful to avoid any compromise with Arianism, which was so prevalent among the Visigoth neighbors.)

Immediately after the first benediction ("The Lord be *always* with you" — "And with your spirit"), there are *three* chants in a row: the *Holy, Holy, Holy* sung in Greek and Latin; then the *Kyrie eleison,* sung by *three* children *three* times; and finally, in alternating verses, the *Benedictus,* the Canticle of Zechariah.

There now follow *three* readings: the Prophets, the Apostles, and the Gospel. After the second reading, the Canticle of the *Three* Children in the Furnace (from chapter *three* in the Book of Daniel) is sung. Then there is a procession for the Gospel. The book is covered with a veil in the Eastern manner, and preceded by a candlestick with seven branches. During this procession the *Holy, Holy, Holy* is repeated.

The sermon is followed by a long litany of petitions, during which the deacon calls upon the faithful from time to time to genuflect (a practice borrowed from the East).

Now there is a new procession, the bringing up of the offerings, while the *Alleluiah* is chanted.

The celebrant now spreads out *three* veils. The first is a tablecloth to cover the altar. The second is what we call the corporal, to receive the host. The third is the veil that covers the chalice and the host, as in the East. An incensing takes place, during which the *Alleluiah* is sung *three* times.

To stress the communion of hearts among all the faithful, there is now the "reading of names" — another Eastern custom. Names of the deceased, including former bishops of the place, are "recommended." Living persons are then named, including the reigning pope. Last come the names of those for whom the Mass is being offered.

Now the assistants exchange the kiss of peace. By custom this kiss is on the lips, a kiss the heart cannot deny.

Finally, with the familiar dialogue, they begin the Preface which concludes with the *Holy, Holy, Holy,* followed this time by a second part, "Blessed is he who comes in the name of the Lord. . . ."

The Mass concludes with the Canticle to the Trinity, and blessed bread is distributed, as in the East, for those who have not received communion.

* * *

This Gallican Mass liturgy has a certain appeal. It is full of imagination and striking detail. Why, then, did it fail to survive, while the Eastern liturgies that inspired it in so many ways did survive?

One answer is: it diversified itself to death with imaginative local customs. To take one example: Pope Pelagius II, in 585, was dumbfounded at Gallic customs such as making hosts in the shape of ears, hands, and mouths, to be distributed to people according to personal merit or according to the type grace they prayed for.

There were attempts at uniformity, but these efforts failed. The primate of Lyons, for instance, tried to introduce his church's liturgy into the dioceses in his care. He did not succeed.

Just before the words of consecration, the Eucharistic

Prayer in the Gallican Mass had "movable prayers" that varied with the time of year. This was a carry-over from earlier days when the celebrant would improvise, as Saint Justin had said, "according to his ability." In the Gallican Mass, the problem with this feature was that it provided an opening for unlimited improvisation in the celebration of local feasts.

In our own century, with books in abundance, there are country churches and poor inner-city parishes that use missals until they are ragged. It is not hard to imagine what priests in sixth-century Gaul had to get by with. In that distant era, getting hold of a liturgical manuscript was a major accomplishment for a local priest, and churches were at the mercy of robbers who would make off with such valuables. Priests had little to fall back on but what they knew by heart.

Unchecked variety and complexity were a source of liturgical vulnerability in ancient Gaul. Those weaknesses could render the liturgy vulnerable today as easily as they did then.

The Roman Sacramentaries

In contrast to the Gallican Mass, the Roman papal Mass underwent a slow evolution. The papal Mass was heavy with pomp and ceremony, with dignitaries playing solemn roles. But it remained dignified and well organized.

From the time of Pope Innocent I at the start of the fifth century, Rome recognized only one Eucharistic Prayer — the Canon. The Canon had no movable parts to be manipulated at will. Even variables like the *Hanc igitur* were fixed in writing and had definite days on which they were used.

Nothing was improvised. Texts and chants were checked in advance. Readers and cantors were assigned. Anyone who took part in the Mass had a defined, prearranged role.

This clear-cut approach appealed to the Gallican clergy. They wanted to copy the Roman Mass in its entirety everywhere in Gaul. We may wonder whether the Gallic people shared their clergy's eagerness to adopt the Roman Mass. In

Rome the people had virtually been reduced to spectators at the papal Mass. They had nothing to say back to the celebrant and had no part in the chant.[2]

The Roman Mass of that period is known to us through books called sacramentaries, offshoots from the works of popes Leo, Gelasius, and Gregory the Great. The editions we possess date from the period we are looking at, the beginning of the High Middle Ages.

The fact that these books exist today is due in great part to countless unknown Gallicans. Out of love for the liturgy, men traveled through forests infested with robbers, scaled steep paths through the Alps to get to the Lombard plains, and then walked for weeks before they reached Rome.

Countless unknown manuscript copyists also deserve our thanks. Conscious of their humble role, these men did not even sign their work. But without them we would know little about ancient Roman liturgy. The originals of the *libelli* they copied have all disappeared. But some of the many copies they made survive. Thanks to them we have the following sacramentaries.

The Leonine. This sacramentary was discovered in Verona, Italy, in the eighteenth century. The manuscript dates from the seventh century. For lack of the copyist's name, scholars call his work "the sacramentary of Verona." The document contains a mixture of Mass prayers copied in Rome for use elsewhere. Scholars believe they discern in it traces of ancient *libelli,* and see it as a traditional stage between primitive manuals and sacramentaries properly so-called. Some of the prayers are from Saint Leo the Great (A.D. 440 to 461). Eighteen of the Masses it contains are attributed to Pope Gelasius (A.D. 492 to 496), and others to Pope Vigilius (A.D. 537 to 555).

The Ancient Gelasian. Recopied in Gaul, probably near Paris in the eighth century, this sacramentary is certainly not from Pope Gelasius (A.D. 492 to 496). One clue is that the Canon is that of Saint Gregory (A.D. 590 to 604). It is basically a Roman sacramentary with elements added in

Gaul. Unlike the Leonine, this Ancient Gelasian reflects not only the papal liturgy but those of other Roman churches and monasteries.

The Recent Gelasian. This collection was very probably drawn up at the Abbey of Flavigny in Burgundy around the year 750. Based on the Ancient Gelasian, this composite collection also makes use of a sacramentary of the Gregorian type, while retaining numerous Gallican prayers. It is this happy mingling that accounted for its popularity. It continued to be recopied and used even after the eighth-century reform of Charlemagne and on into the eleventh century. It was influential right up until the Mass of Pope Saint Pius V in the sixteenth century.

The Gregorian sacramentaries. In spite of their name, none of the Gregorian sacramentaries are by Saint Gregory the Great (A.D. 590 to 604); when his work was recopied, modifications from the copyist's time were always added. The manuscript called the *Paduense* dates from around 650 to 680, only a half century after Gregory, and circulated throughout the West from then on. The eighth-century manuscript called the *Hadrianum* is a copy of a Gregorian sacramentary done in Rome by Pope Adrian I (A.D. 772 to 795) at the explicit request of the Emperor Charlemagne.

Gallican missals. The Gauls had their own local equivalents of Roman sacramentaries. From the eighth century on, we find a Gothic missal, an ancient Gallican missal, a missal for the Franks, and so on. No one of these books was imposed in its region. These collections already contained borrowings from Rome.

Concluding Observations

The sacramentaries are priceless because of the knowledge they afford us. But they are perhaps even more priceless because of what they teach us about their copyists, whose outlook was so characteristic of liturgists in the High Middle Ages:

These liturgists were quite conscious of the defects in the

Gallican liturgies, as well as of the fact that these liturgies were well suited to their Gallican populations.

These liturgists were attracted to the Roman liturgy, which they venerated as being that of the head of the Church. Yet they were sophisticated enough to realize that Roman liturgy could not be imposed, just as it was, upon the Gauls. It had to be adapted before being adopted. The liturgy of Rome, great as it was, was not everyone's cup of tea.

In spite of their great respect for the papal liturgy, the copyists of the sacramentaries did not hesitate to modify it in religious and literary ways. They would transcribe, side by side, liturgical texts that had originated in different periods. And they would modify these texts, adding their own explanations, as if everything came from the same source and was of equal value. They were extremely easygoing in this regard. None of them seems to have felt that any liturgical text, even the Canon, was off limits when it came to making such changes. They simply did not believe that these texts had to remain just as they were throughout the centuries.

Modern scholars who study these documents must use all their ingenuity to sort out all the tangled elements, and then to discover their date, source, and exact meaning. This painstaking work is far from useless. Even with our present post-Vatican II missal, it is never useless to know the antiquity of such and such a prayer — to know that we are praying with Leo, Gelasius, Gregory, Pius V, or...Paul VI. The Spirit will not abandon his Church, even to the end of time.

Notes

1. Albert Rouet, *La Messe dans l'histoire,* Les Editions du Cerf, Paris 1979, pages 96 to 103.
2. Josef A. Jungmann, S.J., *The Mass of the Roman Rite,* Volume One, page 73.

5
Roman Tradition and the Carolingian Renaissance
(A.D. 751 to A.D. 1014)

In the liturgical domain, the end of the first thousand years in the West witnessed a new wave of creativity. Along with a shift in political power, the center of liturgical creativity moved northward from Rome to the land of the Franks, then further north to the Germanic lands. One man dominated the period: *Charlemagne*, the grandson of Charles Martel.

In the year 732, Charles the "Hammer (Martel) of the Infidels" crushed the Saracen invaders at Poitiers. Twenty years later Charles' son, Pepin the Short, took the throne, ending the ineffective reign of the Merovingians. With the approbation of Pope Zachary (A.D. 741 to 752), Pepin was proclaimed King of the Franks.

France was a mosaic of populations more interested in guarding their independence than in forming a strong nation. To weld these groups into political unity, Pepin the Short waged incessant war, putting down one rebellion after another. But Pepin also tried a positive approach. Realizing that religion could be a cohesive element, he strove for liturgical unity among the Gauls.

Liturgical diversity in the region bordered on anarchy. There were some customs that the Gauls had in common, but the dominant pattern was that of the primitive Church: each celebrant organizes his Mass as he understands it, and prays "according to his ability."

Pepin sent copyists to Rome. They came back laden with liturgical documents. It soon was apparent, however, that the Roman liturgies were not adequate for Gaul. The Roman texts were not complete enough, and the solemn Roman approach struck a dead note among the lively Gauls. Being a good psychologist and a skilled politician, Pepin the Short decided not to adopt but to adapt. But who would do the adapting?

Charlemagne and Alcuin

Charlemagne inherited his father Pepin's vast kingdom in the year 768. Up to that time there had been no progress toward liturgical adaptation. But Charlemagne was perceptive enough to see what a powerful instrument the liturgy could be in the cause of political unity. As luck would have it, he met the very man who was able to accomplish the adaptation.

Charlemagne was a friend of Pope Adrian I (A.D. 772 to 795), in whose defense he had put down the Lombards in 774. On his way to Rome in 781 to have his son baptized by the pope (and also to be crowned King of Italy), Charlemagne stopped at Parma. There he met an Anglo-Saxon Benedictine monk, the deacon Alcuin. Alcuin happened to be traveling home from Rome where his bishop had sent him on a mission. The meeting was one of history's happy accidents.

During that period of Latin cultural decline on the Continent, Alcuin had gone to the British Isles and received a classical education second to none. He was also a born educator. In his fifties when he met Charlemagne, Alcuin was Master of the cathedral school in York, England.

Charlemagne offered Alcuin a position as his minister of public education. Alcuin accepted. With permission from his bishop, who lent him to the Continent as a missionary, Alcuin took up residence the following year at Aix-la-Chapelle, Charlemagne's capital.

Being a Benedictine, Alcuin had a personal interest in liturgical books. In preparing Charlemagne's reform, he had copies of all the sacramentaries then known in Gaul: a Gelasian of the ancient type, a Recent Gelasian, a Gregorian of the Padua type, and various Gallican books. But that was not enough for Alcuin. He persuaded Charlemagne to ask Pope Adrian for a copy of the Mass texts used in Rome —

and not just a copy from some Roman church, but a copy of the sacramentary the pope himself used. That way the reform would be under the auspices of the highest authority. The pope went along with it. The book the pope used was the *Hadrianum* — the sacramentary of Gregory the Great with additional prayers from the past two centuries.

Alcuin set about editing the text. He made a slight change in the Canon: each celebrant was now to mention the name of the local bishop and the fact that he was in communion with his fellow bishops — "orthodox defenders of the faith" — a carry-over from the old fights against Arianism.

He also added a long Supplement from other sacramentaries. For example, he added beautiful prayers for ordinary Sundays from the Ancient Gelasian and some occasional Masses, notably Masses for the dead, which were not found in the Roman sacramentary. (When the pope honored a church by celebrating Mass there, it was never a Mass for the dead.)

Alcuin deliberately borrowed little from Gallican texts. He put in Gregorian chant everywhere, replacing Gallican chants. But to make sure that there would be participation by the people, Charlemagne had Alcuin stipulate that everyone was to chant the *Gloria Patri* and the *Sanctus*. Charlemagne was intent on creating unity among peoples.

The Fate of Alcuin's Reform

Charlemagne published Alcuin's new *Hadrianum* in 789. Immediately, Gallican copyists began to take liberties with the text. Alcuin had been careful to make his important Supplement a separate section from the original Roman sections. Copyists of the text did not show the same scruple. Manuscripts began to circulate in which, for the convenience of Mass celebrants, parts of Alcuin's Supplement were inserted within Pope Adrian's collection.

Charlemagne had declared Alcuin's *Hadrianum* the only official liturgical text in his kingdom. Nevertheless, the Recent Gelasian, a Burgundian collection that borrowed heavily from Gallican liturgies, continued to be very popular. These two currents — Alcuin's *Hadrianum* and the Recent Gelasian — ended up merging into what might be called a Franco-Roman liturgy.

This new hybrid liturgy sealed the fate of the purely Gallican liturgies, which were already on the decline. But at the same time the new hybrid liturgy modified the liturgy of Rome itself. In a strange reversal, the new Franco-Roman Mass would return to Rome via the Germanic states and reshape Roman liturgy in the style of a Germano-Roman Mass. Before we examine this reversal, let us look at the liturgical customs born from the merger of Roman tradition and Carolingian vitality. The entire medieval Mass tradition was a product of this merger.

Elements of the Franco-Roman Mass

The prayers. Roman prayers were generally in the plural. People said "We," expressing the concerns of the whole Church. In contrast, very many of the prayers composed in Gaul were in the singular as if they were private prayers of the priest.

This style was evident at the beginning of Mass in the *"I* confess to Almighty God" and "through *my* fault . . . *my* most grievous fault." The prayer by the priest at the Offertory said: "Holy Father . . . accept this immaculate host that *I*, Your unworthy servant, am offering to You, *my* true and living God." The same individual prayer form was used in various other places in the Mass.

Was this style due to the fact that these prayers were now reserved to the priest alone and recited in a low voice? Or was it a sign of a narrow individualistic preoccupation? Perhaps it was more. It also may have been a sign of another *sensitivity,* a need for direct intimacy with the Lord. In the Psalms, for example, people recognize themselves when the Psalmist says "I" — "Bless the Lord, O my soul" or "He only is my rock and my salvation." Jungmann observes: "The restlessness and agitation, the strong passionate estheticism which mark the German character, must have been the Celt's too, but only in greater measure, and so were found already well suited to the Gallican liturgy. This liturgy continued in force and did not give way before the Roman till it had communicated to it something of its own stamp."[1] He hits the nail right on the head.

Communion rites. People continued to receive Communion under both forms. But from the eleventh century on, the use of unleavened bread prevailed. According to Jungmann, "Alcuin and his pupil Rabanus Maurus are the first indisputable witnesses to this new practice . . . ."[2]

Soon the host became thin, round, and white. Its small size now made it less convenient to receive in the hand. So it was judged more proper and respectful to receive it directly on the tongue. Receiving it on the tongue was easier if the communicant knelt, which was also a sign of respect. And to make the genuflection easier, an arm rest was developed — the communion rail. So, little by little, new liturgical customs came into being. Though none of them was from early Church practice and none of them was Roman in origin, Rome later adopted them.

During this same period, people developed the unfortunate custom of going to Communion less and less.

The altar. Separation of the celebrant from the people was stressed more and more. Jungmann states: "The altar was moved back to the rear wall of the apse."[3] The sanctuaries in these northern churches were turned toward the East and that was the direction the priest faced when he prayed. So he had to have his back to the people. As a result, all that people saw was a priest in the distance making mysterious gestures.

Liturgical gestures. There was a great deal of multiple gesturing — multiple signs of the cross, blessings, and incensing. There were also multiple kisses — kissing of the altar, the Gospel book, and the paten — and multiple bows and genuflections. Elevating the host became a popular feature because people no longer received Communion but wanted to "see the host." All of these gestures originated in

Gallic lands and became part of Roman practice.

Liturgical vestments. The stole was not a Roman vestment. But in Spain and Gaul, as in the East, it was the distinctive insignia of deacons. Priests also wore stoles but in a different manner. The stole was eventually adopted in Rome.

The Franco-Germanic use of the cope made its way to Rome. In various ceremonies it took the place of the chasuble.

The wearing of a ring by a bishop was used in seventh-century Spain. From there the practice passed into Gaul, then into Germany, and finally to Rome.

The use of the mitre went the opposite way. It was the ordinary headdress of the pope in Rome, and in Gaul it became the liturgical headdress of the bishop.

Bells. In the West a place famous for the making of bells was the Campania region. The Spanish word *campana* means "bell," and the French word *campanile* — "bell tower" — is a derivative. From the start of the ninth century, the use of bells was common throughout Gaul. In Rome wooden clappers were preferred, as a means of calling people to church services. The bell finally won out over the clapper in Rome, and Mass servers began to use small bells at the foot of the altar.

The organ. The first organ came from the East; it was offered by the court of Constantinople to Pepin the Short around the middle of the eighth century. A few years later, Charlemagne had an organ built in his private chapel to enhance the liturgy there. That is where liturgical organ music began in the West. So organ music, which is so closely associated with the "traditional" Roman Mass, is not really a Roman legacy at all.

The missal. Prayers in the first person singular were a feature of Celtic and Northern piety. That is a feature, one might think, that Rome did not have to adopt. After all, it was the Gauls who went to Rome to copy texts, and not vice versa. But the truth is that the missal, the "Roman" model of liturgical books, came from the North.

In earlier centuries celebrants, readers, and cantors each had a text for their role in the Mass. No one needed to have all of the texts in a single volume. But in the private Mass of Franco-Germanic devotion, the celebrant did have to have at his disposal the Ordinary of the Mass, the readings, and in some cases even the chants. And these were packaged for the private celebrant all in a single volume — the missal. This complete missal appeared in the eleventh century, and Rome adopted it!

The Roman court was in a state of complete disintegration, and reduced to asking Germanic monasteries for their liturgical books. "It would seem that at that time new manuscripts were simply not being produced. In the scriptoria of the North, on the contrary, there was bustling activity; in particular there flourished at the time in German monasteries the art of manuscript illumination."[4] Here is how the strange reversal took place: ". . . Pope Gregory V made an agreement in 998 with the abbey of Reichenau, stipulating that in return for certain privileges accorded on the occasion of the blessing of a new abbot, the monks were to send, amongst other things, a new sacramentary. It goes without saying that this would mean only the style of Mass book then current in the North."[5]

The sacramentaries of 998 would turn into missals before very long.

The *Credo* Affair

This affair provides a good example of how a prayer came to be part of the Mass. It also highlights Charlemagne's role and shows the influence of Germanic politics in Rome.

We are all familiar with the two Creeds: the Apostles' Creed (which many people say as part of their morning or evening prayers) and the Nicene Creed (which is usually said or sung at Sunday Masses and on feast days). In the beginning, both of these Creeds were professions of faith used by *individuals* about to be baptized (which accounts for the fact that the singular is used). Neither Creed was part of the Mass.

The Apostles' Creed, which is shorter and more succinct, was composed and used for baptismal ceremonies in Rome.

The Nicene Creed was hammered out as a reaction to heresies in the East. This is the one we are concerned with here.

Timothy, the Patriarch of Constantinople (A.D. 511-517), was the first to order this long Creed to be professed at every solemn Mass. His example was soon followed throughout the East. It was recited just before the kiss of peace preceding Communion,[6] as if to show that all were going to Communion with the same faith.

From there this Creed took root in Spain. The Byzantines occupied a coastal region there and had naturally brought their Eastern customs with them. In 589, the Visigoth King Reccared decided to have the Nicene Creed recited at every Mass, still before Communion, but at the end of the Canon before the *Pater noster.*

From Spain, it appears that the custom crossed over to Ireland and then to England. From there, Alcuin — the former Master of the cathedral school in York — introduced it to Charlemagne for use in the Mass.[7] And that is how Charlemagne came to adopt the Nicene Creed at Mass in his chapel. He decided to have it sung right after the Gospel, as a ratification of the faith that had just been proclaimed. (That way it would be recited by the many whose practice it was to slip away before Communion time.)

Charlemagne's use of the Creed at Mass was so novel that it sparked a long debate in Rome.

Charlemagne was skilled in having things his way despite all of Rome's authority. In the first round of debate, he succeeded in getting his way with Pope Leo III. The pope insisted on one restriction: the Creed was to be said only on Sundays and major feast days. It was not, after all, a properly Eucharistic prayer.

But then the debate flared up again for another reason. In still another private initiative, Charlemagne introduced the term *filioque* — "and from the Son" — into the Nicene Creed. This word added the idea that in the Trinity, the Holy Spirit proceeds not from the Father only, but from the Father *and* the Son.

This idea was not new. The *filioque* had already been added to the Creed in Spain at the insistence of the Council of Toledo in 589, and had caused no ripples in Rome. But Charlemagne's decision to have the word *filioque* sung in his imperial chapel raised the matter to a new level.

The pope was actually not opposed to the *filioque* doctrine. But singing it out loud in the Creed was a different matter. This could only anger the Greeks, who considered the wording inexact. The Greeks preferred to say that the Holy Spirit proceeds from the Father *through* the Son, and not *from* the Son.

The matter might have escaped having major repercussions if it had been kept low key. But in Jerusalem, right in the center of Greek influence, Frankish monks began expressing their conviction in the matter by crying out *"filioque"* in loud voices. The pope protested vigorously. But Charlemagne continued to have the *filioque* sung, and the custom gradually spread throughout Frankish and Germanic lands.

That is where the matter stood until Emperor Henry II went to Rome in 1014 and was shocked to hear Masses with no Creed. In vain Roman clerics explained that the Roman Church had never been tainted by heresies and had no need for constant proclamations of faith. The holy emperor (later canonized a saint in 1146) was not swayed by these explanations. He expressed his scandal with such force that Pope Benedict VIII finally capitulated. And so the Creed was officially introduced into Western liturgy.[8]

Here was a case in which the whole Church — East and West, people and pope — played a role in introducing the Creed into the Mass.

From the Franco-Roman
to the Germano-Roman Mass

The encounter between Roman tradition and the Carolingian renaissance brings out three valuable lessons.

The first lesson emerges from the genuine crossbreeding born of the north-south movement — or, if you prefer, the movement from center to periphery and back to center. It was a true crossbreeding. As Jungmann notes, "Out of all this shaping and shifting of liturgical forms in the Carolingian area a new Mass rite of the Roman-Frankish type was produced. It was at once rich and sharply outlined and soon had won wide acceptance."[9]

Its acceptance was so great that it altered "the entire subsequent history of the Roman liturgy. About the middle of the tenth century the Roman liturgy began to return in force from Franco-Germanic lands to Italy and to Rome. . . . This importation entailed supplanting the local form of the Roman liturgy by its Gallicized version, even at the very center of Christendom."[10]

Here indeed is an excellent lesson in favor of communion between churches. Let no church say of another: I do not need you.

The second lesson lies in the undeniable success of the liturgical reform that Pepin the Short envisioned, Charlemagne made a reality, and his successors continued. The emperor's messengers no doubt kept an eye out for the correct performance of Sunday Masses. But acceptance of the reform seems to have been voluntary. People and clergy alike felt the need of a reform to counteract the anarchy and disintegration in Gallican liturgies from the Merovingian period.

The main reason for success, perhaps, was that people saw in the balanced reform that was put before them a reflection of their own tastes and customs. In a liturgical reform, written texts are important. But the ambience, the context, also makes a difference. And of even greater importance are the spirit, the culture, the peculiar human and Christian "feel" that flow from a people's long experience.

The third lesson lies in the fact that the success of the reform grew out of a wasted opportunity. Back in the time of Pope Saint Callistus in the third century, the Roman Church abandoned Greek and adopted Latin so that ordinary people could understand the liturgy. But the Latin Mass which so attracted Charlemagne was pretty well limited to Rome before he transplanted it among the Franks and the Germans. When that transplant took place, a golden opportunity was wasted, critics claim. The use of Gallican languages, instead of Latin, could have been the salvation of the disintegrating Gallican liturgies.

Just as missionaries in Africa today are doing, Holy Scripture could have been translated into the various Gallican tongues, thereby creating new written languages and the basis of new liturgical languages. That this is not a utopian idea is borne out by the fact that a short while later in the mid-ninth century, saints Cyril and Methodius conducted services, including the Roman Mass, among the Slavs in the Slavic tongue. German clerics were the bitterest opponents of the two saints, alleging that they "dared conduct divine worship in a *lingua barbarica,* whereas in accordance with the inscription on the Cross, this should be done only *hebraice, graece et latine''* — in Hebrew, Greek, and Latin.[11] That arbitrary reference to John 19:20 appears to rule out nothing less than Pentecost itself!

Before long, the common people themselves did not understand Latin even in Rome. So, by the end of the first thousand years of Christianity, an unprecedented revolution was in full swing. The only ones who understood the language of the Mass were clerics. "A new kind of *disciplina arcani* or discipline of the secret had developed, a concealment of things holy, not from the heathen — there were none — but from the Christian people themselves."[12]

This forgetting of the principle of Pope Callistus did not take place without serious drawbacks, as we will see. Protestantism did not wait another thousand years before demanding the Scriptures and the prayers of Eucharistic celebration in understandable language.

Notes

1. Josef A. Jungmann, S.J., *The Mass of the Roman Rite,* Volume One, page 77.
2. Jungmann, Volume One, page 84.
3. Jungmann, Volume One, page 83.
4. Jungmann, Volume One, page 96.
5. Jungmann, Volume One, page 96.
6. Jungmann, Volume One, page 468.
7. Jungmann, Volume One, page 469.
8. Jungmann, Volume One, pages 469-470.
9. Jungmann, Volume One, page 92.
10. Jungmann, Volume One, page 95.
11. Jungmann, Volume One, page 81.
12. Jungmann, Volume One, page 81.

6
The Gothic Mass
(A.D. 1014 to A.D. 1517)

In the year 1014, the Nicene Creed became part of the Roman Mass at the insistence of the saintly Emperor Henry II — a clear case of northern influence on Rome.

In the year 1517, 500 years later, a German monk named Martin Luther initiated sweeping reforms in opposition to Roman practice.

These two events define the time frame of this next period in the history of the Mass.

As a term describing the Mass in these centuries, the word *Gothic* is ambivalent. To some, "Gothic" connotes splendid cathedrals, the ultimate in architecture at Paris, Rheims, Cologne, and Chartres. It also connotes a theological edifice built by that peerless master, Saint Thomas Aquinas.

For others, "Gothic" evokes a barbarian world cloaked in centuries of darkness which produced nothing to rival the civilized art of Greece and Rome. To which category did the Gothic Mass belong?

In this period there was amazingly little development in the area of liturgy, especially in comparison to the bold and creative work going on in architecture and theology. The liturgy displayed its pageantry in marvelous buildings that drew fascinated crowds. Theologians and poets endowed the liturgy with magnificent hymns. Gregorian music gave birth to masterpieces. But with all that, the liturgy was dissipating its vital sap on excess foliage.

Eminent professors scrutinized the dogmatic rationale of the Mass with vigor and precision. Gothic liturgists, following the trend of popular piety, lost themselves in a cloud of rubrics and allegories. The liturgy, meanwhile, did little more than give rise to popular devotions, some of them lapsing into deviations.

As Jungmann notes, there was "no cutting back to the living roots, no springing forth of new, healthy growths. Scholastic theology produced nothing for the liturgy of the Mass or for a better understanding of it."[1]

Low Masses

Low Masses usurped more and more of a place in popular devotion. People were convinced of the priceless value of the Eucharistic sacrifice. So, very rightly, they asked that it be celebrated for their personal intentions and for their deceased.

Unfortunately, however, some people began to think of numbers and repetition in terms that bordered on magic. The greatest importance was attributed to the number of Masses. It was particularly effective, so they believed, to have Masses for the dead celebrated on several days in a row. "Series are stipulated for 3, 5, 7, 9 and 30 Masses, even for 41, 44, or 45 . . . sometimes, too, a specified number of candles and a specified number of alms-gifts are stipulated. What was really questionable in this practice of Mass series and Votive Masses was the assurance — recurring time and time again — of unfailing results."[2]

Soon, on weekdays, Masses for the dead supplanted all other types of Masses. As a result, the annual liturgical cycle was neglected.

What we see here are the beginnings of deviations which could give rise to discord in the sixteenth century.

The Movements of the Priest

Solemn Mass continued to be the most important, but people now considered it a spectacle unfolding before their eyes. This attitude accounted for the multiplying of visible rites.

The repetition of signs of the cross and kissings of the altar has already been mentioned. From now on, the celebrant would read the Epistle at the right side of the altar, and the Gospel at the left side. This practice gave spectators — which is what they were called — a clue to what part of the Mass the priest was at. To provide room for the missal at both sides, altars had to be lengthened. Up to that time, the altar was scarcely a yard square in size.

But why have the Gospel said at the left side of the altar? An allegorical explanation was ready at hand: God, in Old Testament times, had addressed himself to the just — on the right. Now, in these Gospel times, God deigns to show his merciful favor to pagans and sinners — on the left.

From time to time the celebrant would turn to face the people. How many times? Five? That must be because Christ appeared five times after his Resurrection.

So much for allegory. Rubrics also had a field day. The celebrant extends his hands. How far? Rubricians determined exactly how far and how high the priest should extend his hands. The priest touched the consecrated host. There had to be a genuflexion before and a genuflexion after.

The number of prayers also grew to excess. In Rome they limited themselves to one, two, or at the most three prayers in a row. In Gaul the sky was the limit. The only obligation was to make it an uneven number. Some priests went so far as to have five, nine, and fifteen prayers in a row.

In the midst of all this proliferation, Saint Thomas Aquinas remained moderate and realistic in his explanation of the Mass.[3]

The Real Presence and Contemplation of the Host

The two basic elements of the Mass — sacrifice and the gift of Christ as food — were undisputed realities for Christians in the Middle Ages. Theological reflection deepened and affirmed the two elements ever more forcefully. In the twelfth century Anselm of Laon (d. 1117) and William of Champeaux (d. 1121) stated with clear precision that, in the Eucharist, not only the Body and Blood of Christ but the whole Christ is present. Meanwhile, however, the neo-Manichean heresy of the Albigensians was openly scorning the Mass and denying the Real Presence. The faithful reacted sharply to this heresy by affirming the Real Presence, and they wanted to express their faith by contemplating Christ concealed under the appearance of bread.[4]

The desire to view the sacred species gave birth to the practice of elevating the host and chalice after the two consecrations at Mass. Before the consecration the priest would take the bread in his hands and elevate it slightly. The people attached great importance to this gesture because it allowed them to see the host, though only a little; the priest had his back to the people. The problem with this custom was that it risked creating an ill-advised respect; the unconsecrated host was still only bread. To avoid the problem, in the year 1210 the bishop of Paris ordered priests to elevate the host only *after* the consecration, but to raise it high enough at that time so that the faithful could easily see it and venerate Christ present in the host.[5] A few years later, priests would also begin to elevate the chalice.

For many of the faithful, contemplation of the sacred host after the consecration became *the* essential devotion of the Mass. Merely seeing the consecrated host brought peace of mind; a person could be sure he would not die suddenly on any day he had seen the sacred host. In cities people rushed from church to church to see the consecrated host as often as possible. They looked for locations in church that would give them a better view of the altar. In some parishes, we are told, most of the people would enter the church at the bell before the consecration and race out immediately afterward.

In England people would cry out to a celebrant who was not raising the host high enough: "Higher, Sir John, higher!"[6]

Even the least devout were serious about seeing the host. A story from the twelfth century goes: "Raymond, an anticlerical peasant, could not go to Mass because he refused to pay the tithe. In a fit of rage, he declared: 'We must destroy all the churches.' Why? 'Mass would then be celebrated in the open fields, and all those who wanted to could see the Body of the Lord.' "

To counteract this tendency of the people, some priests began to have several elevations during Mass, a custom that gave us a small elevation at the end of the Canon, at the *Per ipsum,* and before Communion at the *Agnus Dei.*[7]

This same devotion took another form. The feast of Corpus Christi was instituted in 1246, and the Blessed Sacrament began to be carried in a monstrance (from the Latin verb *monstrare* — to show) in triumphal processions through cities and towns. The monstrance was on display during the high Mass after the procession, then during the eight days following. Finally, despite Roman reluctance, the practice of celebrating Mass before the exposed Blessed Sacrament became widespread. After the Lutheran reform, this devotion took on new strength in protest against that reform.

Communion During Mass

The practice of Communion under both species continued during the thirteenth century, but little by little it disappeared. At the end it was done only at the coronation of emperors and kings. Louis XIV was probably the last king to communicate under both species. Communion with only the host was already infrequent and the practice continued to decline. Many of the faithful received Communion only as Viaticum.

In the thirteenth century a reaction set in. Theologians and mystics urged the importance of Communion for all the faithful. But the opposite habit was so deeply ingrained that if people wanted to go to Communion during Mass, the rite was tacked on like a foreign element that did not really belong there; priests used the special rite of Communion for the sick!

As late as the 1950s, the following scenario was not uncommon. After the priest received Communion, the Mass server looked out toward the body of the church. If anyone was approaching the communion rail, the server rang the little bell and began to recite *"Confiteor Deo omnipotenti. . . ."* The flow of the Mass was interrupted to make room for the Communion of the faithful as though it were not a normal part of the Mass. The practice was not exactly a remembrance of the Last Supper invitation, "Take and eat."

Singing and Ornaments

In the twelfth and thirteenth centuries, Gregorian chant became the business of the clergy and the choir. The people had no part in it. As the chants in the Ordinary of the Mass became more splendid, the role of the choir became more and more important.

Melodies for the *Kyrie, Sanctus,* and *Agnus Dei* became widespread. At first, each one was an independent composition. Then they became matching parts of a whole. The most ancient example of a sung Mass is the Mass of the Angels, which appeared in the thirteenth century and won popular approval. The sung *Gloria* soon joined the *Kyrie, Sanctus,* and *Agnus Dei* as part of the series.

It was in France that the first sung Masses in the modern sense came into being. They were composed in polyphony and no longer linked to or dependent on Gregorian melodies. The use of the word *Mass* for musical compositions was significant; people now went to "hear" the Mass.

This is also the period during which the organ reached its peak of perfection, earning it a place in large churches everywhere.[8]

The priest's vestments and the altar became more ornate. Around the year 1200, Pope Innocent III assigned liturgical colors for the various Masses: white for ordinary feasts; red for Pentecost and feasts of martyrs; black for days of penance and Masses for the dead; green for ordinary days.

The chasuble became more and more ornate; the ample, flowing chasuble of former days was rarely worn. Chasubles acquired a stiff lining, giving artists full scope for painting and embroidering them.[9]

At this same time the altar table, which had already been lengthened, gained an ornamental screen at the back — the reredos. The screens were gradually built higher and higher and decorated with sculptures and paintings.

People might not have been able to understand what was said at Mass, but they had plenty to see.

Concluding Remarks

In the Middle Ages, liturgy in the West was dominated by the blending of Roman tradition with the Franco-German liturgy of the Mass. This blending was desired, perhaps necessary, and certainly successful. But it came about at the expense of the use of living languages; it blocked the people from intelligent, in-depth participation in the Mass. Consequently, the importance of details about decor and surface matters of ceremony was blown out of proportion. This tendency accounted for the triumph of variety over the perfect unity once dreamed of by Charlemagne. In the thirteenth century, the variety of practices and diocesan books had no limit.[10] It is no surprise that Jungmann points to a "springing of the old grooves" as characteristic of the Gothic age.[11]

Looking at this emphasis on surface matters in all their variety at the expense of what is more basic, we can begin to understand Pope Pius V's *unifying* reform.

Notes

1. Josef A. Jungmann, S.J., *The Mass of the Roman Rite*, Volume One, page 128.
2. Jungmann, Volume One, page 130.
3. A.-G. Martimort, ed., *The Church at Prayer, Volume 2: The Eucharist*, pages 49-50 (Herder and Herder, 1973).
4. Jungmann, Volume One, pages 118-119.
5. Jungmann, Volume One, page 120.
6. Jungmann, Volume One, page 121, note 101.
7. Jungmann, Volume One, page 121.
8. Jungmann, Volume One, page 126.
9. Jungmann, Volume One, page 112.
10. Martimort, Volume 2, page 50.
11. Jungmann, Volume One, page 103.

PART THREE
The Mass in the Modern Era
(A.D. 1517 to the Present Day)

7 The Mass of Saint Pius V

8 From the Council of Trent to Vatican II

9 The Choice of Vatican II and the Missal of Paul VI

7
The Mass of Saint Pius V

The phrase "Autumn of the Middle Ages" describes the fourteenth and fifteenth centuries. It also describes the liturgy of the period, especially the Gothic Mass. There was "no springing forth of new, healthy growths."

But in every other area the fourteenth and fifteenth centuries were bursting into bloom. Europe was multiplying its contacts in Africa and the Far East. It was discovering America; Columbus reached Cuba and Haiti in 1492 and the Continent in 1498.

Toward the middle of the fifteenth century, Gutenburg put the finishing touches on his printing machine. One of the first great works to be done on it was the Bible, which came off the press in 1455. The Bible in print! Now the possibility could be entertained of putting the Bible into everyone's hands, translated into every language under the sun. (Between the years 1466 and 1520, forty-five versions of the Bible did in fact appear in German and French.)

The Roman Church, meanwhile, had barely recovered from a long illness. The exile of the papacy at Avignon (1309 to 1376) had no sooner ended when the ugly wound of the Great Schism (1378 to 1417) tore the Church apart. Three popes were reigning at the same time, Saint Catherine of Siena giving allegiance to one and Saint Vincent Ferrer upholding another. For the Church it was a somber time indeed.

But the Church's crowning misfortune at the end of the fifteenth century was the scandalous depravity of the papal court. For fear of a new schism, no one made any effort to depose the Borgia pope, Alexander VI (1492 to 1503), a remarkably intelligent but dissolute man.

The successors of Alexander VI — Julius II (1503 to 1513) and Leo X (1513 to 1521) — were admirable patrons of the arts. Masterpieces of architecture, sculpture, and painting were being produced. It was the age of Michelangelo, Raphael, and Leonardo da Vinci.

The liturgy came to the fore, but only to split the West in two. One camp opted for innovation, which they called the true tradition, as a way of coping with the new times. Rome, the other camp, was trying hard to put its affairs in order.

The Church was sprouting saints and missionaries — Ignatius of Loyola and Francis Xavier, soon to be joined by Jean de Brébeuf and Isaac Jogues. There were mystics — John of the Cross, Teresa of Avila, the missionary-mystic Marie of the Incarnation, and others.

But to this Renaissance world in springtime, Rome could find nothing more to offer than the Gothic Mass. It had been pruned of some excess foliage, but it was still "the Autumn Mass."

The missal of Pope Saint Pius V would be Rome's answer to Luther's protest.

Martin Luther Enters the Picture

There is no need here to go into Luther's enormous influence on religion and civil affairs in the sixteenth century. But we will outline his position concerning the Mass because some defensive decisions about liturgy were made by the Council of Trent and Pope Pius V in reaction to Luther's ideas and practices.

Luther was protesting against true abuses in the area of indulgences. But he also leveled severe criticism at the Mass. In his view, the way the Mass was understood and celebrated was all too often nothing more than superstition. (We have to ask whether Luther was all wrong. Some clergymen at the time were persuading people — their fee providers — that "during Mass one does not grow old"; "during Mass one will never fall ill"; "during Mass your deceased relatives have their suffering in purgatory suspended"; and so on. All this was put in print at Strasbourg in the year 1504 in the *Summula Raymundi*.)

Perhaps he did not make himself clear. His language was

certainly outrageous. But Luther was protesting against the idea that the Mass is a true sacrifice in the sense that it repeats the once and for all sacrifice of Christ *as if Christ's sacrifice were not sufficient*. No Catholic theologian would have wanted to defend the idea Luther was attacking. But on the other hand, did not Jesus himself ask us to make our own his sacrifice on the Cross by doing "this in remembrance of" his Last Supper?

Other reformers denied the Real Presence; Luther believed in it. But he did not believe in devotion to the Real Presence outside the celebration of the Last Supper.

Luther violently opposed the practice of Mass stipends, which some of the clergy and people were abusing. He even attacked the practice of private Masses. He was a passionate advocate of salvation by faith alone *(sola fides)* and wanted preaching of the Word nourished by Scripture alone *(sola Scriptura)* to have first place in the liturgy.

Finally, Luther stressed that the liturgy belongs to the people, that Baptism makes us a priestly people. So, as early as the year 1526, Luther recommended that the liturgy be prayed and sung in German.

In Germany this reformed worship became thoroughly German. In Sweden it became Swedish; in England, English; and in France, French. In each nation worship took on the cultural form of the people.

Luther, in other words, called for a return to the principle of Pope Saint Callistus. But wasn't this a threat to the one, true teaching of the Church? Wasn't that teaching already in jeopardy?

The Council of Trent and the Liturgy

As far back as 1518, Luther had advocated a new ecumenical council. The recent Fifth Lateran Council, which lasted from 1512 to 1517, had not been able to tackle the real problems. Rome hesitated. But finally, in 1542, Pope Paul III ventured to convoke a council in the little town of Trent, Italy. Although it was interrupted several times — King

Francis I of France was still at war with Emperor Charles V —
the Council of Trent went on from 1545 through 1562,
holding as many as twenty-five sessions. The accomplish-
ments of this council were of prime importance. Trent was
the start of what would be called the Counter-Reformation,
which shaped Catholicism for practically four centuries,
right up to Vatican II in the 1960s.

Trent's reform of the Mass tried to squelch Protestant
errors in order to hold onto the liturgical accretions of recent
centuries. There was no inclination to recover the springtime
of the great Patristic centuries, the Golden Age. Among
other things, Trent maintained:

— Christ remains in the consecrated host, even after the
Mass is over (Session Thirteen, Canon 6).

— Adoration of Christ in the Eucharist is legitimate;
therefore, so are processions of the Blessed Sacrament
(Session Thirteen, Canon 6).

— Communion under both species is not necessary in
order to receive Christ whole and entire (Session Twenty-
one, Canons 1 and 2).

— The Mass is truly the sacrifice of Christ (Session
Twenty-two, Canons 1, 3, and 4).

— The Mass may be offered for the living and for the
dead (Session Twenty-two, Canon 3).

— Christ ordained priests to offer his Body and his
Blood (Session Twenty-two, Canon 2).

— The Canon of the Mass contains no errors, and does
not need to be abrogated (Session Twenty-two, Canon 6).

— Ceremonies, vestments, and gestures used in the
Mass do not run counter to true piety (Session Twenty-
two, Canon 7).

— The custom of pronouncing a part of the Canon and
the words of consecration in a low tone is not to be
condemned, nor must it be affirmed that Mass should be
celebrated only in the vernacular language (Session
Twenty-two, Canon 9).

After considering a practical reform of the liturgy, the

Council decided it would get bogged down if it launched into such a complex project; things had already dragged on too long. So it left implementation of the liturgical renewal up to the pope.

Pope Saint Pius V

The reigning pope was Pius IV. He died shortly after naming a commission to carry out the Council's directives. Pius V succeeded him in 1566.

Pius V, Antonio Ghislieri, was born into a family of humble means in Bosco, near Alessandro, in the north of Italy. At only fifteen years of age, Antonio entered the Dominican order. He became so famous in the fight against Protestant errors that he was named Inquisitor General of Christianity by Pope Paul IV. When Paul IV died, Antonio Ghislieri was elected pope by unanimous vote. He was widely known for his austerity of life, absolute integrity, and great goodness to the poor.

Without delay, Pius V began the work of liturgical reform. As he saw it, the most urgent task was the revision of the missal. Even before the Council, there had been calls here and there for a new missal. But the nature of the changes called for differed from country to country. Spain and Portugal, for example, wanted one missal for the entire Western Church. France and England wanted a separate missal for each country.[1]

Pius V opted for *one missal*. Once that was decided, he had a variety of ways to bring it about:

— Being aware of all the changes that had crept in, he could plan an entirely new missal. This missal would contain all new prayers based on Scripture and attuned to the needs and outlook of the time.

— Or, less boldly, he might respond to present needs by a careful selection of time-honored prayers. The new collection would be a sort of prayer synthesis of the centuries. (This option would delight the Renaissance spirit, which reveled in rediscovering antiquity.)

— Or, he might choose a more prudent and time-saving option: select a Mass type from an already existing missal, simplify it, and impose it on the whole Church.

Pius opted for this last kind of reform, and his missal was in print as early as the year 1570. The work that went into it was praiseworthy. But . . . .

The New Missal

The commission authorized by Pius V in 1564 did not look far afield. As the groundwork for their revision they took the *Missal according to the observance of the Roman Curia.*[2]

The missal had this advantage: the texts, ceremonies, language, and chants in it had been honed and polished a long time before, and they formed a solid, coherent whole. No lengthy research was needed, no interminable discussions that would mean putting off the needed reform to some indefinite future time.

Besides, they said, this Mass has the patent of nobility. In the introduction to the decree, they boasted that they could vouch for the fact that this Mass went back to earliest antiquity, because Rome's principle had always been to hold fast to ancient observances as much as possible. (We will see later what this really means.)

Their tendency was to mistrust innovations. In reaction to the liberties advocated by Luther, they defended what they had received and limited themselves to two very small modifications:

— They adopted the *double* elevation. The Curia had been satisfied with just the elevation of the host. The commission felt it was necessary to focus on the presence of the precious Blood, and to hold it up for the adoration of the faithful.

— The curial Mass did not contain an *Ite missa est*. Why have a dismissal rite when the faithful had already left church and were no longer there to dismiss? The *Ite missa est* was put into the missal of Pius V, but before the last blessing. Was this an oversight, or was it a remembrance of the time when the pope would bless people on his way down the aisle as he was leaving? The result in an ordinary Mass was a bit odd. First, the priest tells the people to go — *Ite*. Then he turns toward the altar and prays for a moment or two — the *Placeat*. Then, as though it were an afterthought, he turns around again and blesses people who supposedly have already left.

The commission was much busier pruning than adding. In this regard it showed courage. It suppressed countless votive Masses, some of which bordered on superstition. It suppressed feasts of saints canonized by popular piety in the Middle Ages, as well as many sequences it considered too recent. It also deleted invocations to Mary that had been added to the *Gloria in excelsis* on feasts of the Blessed Virgin — for example: "For you alone are the Holy One, *you who sanctify Mary;* you alone are the Lord, *you who crowned Mary;* you alone are the Most High, *you who govern Mary,* Jesus Christ, with the Holy Spirit, in the glory of God the Father."

In other words, Rome chose moderation.

The Promulgation of the Missal of Pius V

On July 14, 1570, the pope made the new missal official. He did it so forcefully and clearly that no loopholes were left. The Bull of introduction laid down the following rules:

• The missal was obligatory *for the entire Church,* except for dioceses and religious orders which had had their own liturgy for at least 200 years.

• The missal was *unalterable*. It was forbidden to add, subtract, or change anything whatever. It was absolutely forbidden to have the missal printed by any but authorized printers. Therefore, it was also forbidden ever to use any language other than Latin. (This point went far beyond the Council's reservations on the subject of vernacular languages.)

• Celebrants were ordered to use this missal *as soon as possible*. Delays for putting it into practice were restricted to those that were absolutely unavoidable. It allowed:

— one month for the Roman Curia;

— three months for those on the Roman side of the Alps;

— six months for those north of the Alps.

• This ordinance was *forever,* in perpetuity.

• Finally, sanctions and dire threats were directed against anyone defiant enough to dare contravene any of the above decisions. The Bull stated: "If someone dares to change anything, let him know that he incurs immediate excommunication and other possible punishments, that he incurs also the indignation of Almighty God and of the blessed apostles Peter and Paul!"

This categorical imposition was something new. Never before had any pope taken similar measures. Jungmann sees here "the greatest and most consequential innovation of the Mass book of Pius V."[3]

Why was Pius V so adamant? The reasons are not hard to guess:

— The main reason was probably the fear of falling back into a liturgy that would be diversified to the point of anarchy, ushering in all sorts of heretical errors and abuses flowing from the spirit of the times.

— The pope also probably hoped that a tight rein on the printing of the book would ensure an error-free missal. Even careful copyists made errors, sometimes serious ones. Careful control of the printing process did in fact play an essential role in the success of this unifying project.

Was It a True Reform?

The medieval Mass was a crossbreed of Roman and Carolingian elements heavily overlaid with Gothic rites. Did the pruning done by Pius V's commission really reform the Mass? Let us consider the facts.

There was no great gap between the missal of 1570 and that of 1474, the year when the *Missal for the use of the Roman Curia* was first printed in Milan. A simple comparison of the two books speaks for itself. According to

Father Adrien Nocent, "What some call the missal of Saint Pius V is not really his, because though that pope promulgated it, it existed a century before that promulgation. A simple reading suffices to convince a person that very few changes were made to the missal of 1474 by the commission formed by Saint Pius V."[4]

The Milanese missal of 1474 repeated what Pope Nicholas III had prescribed for observance in Rome in the year 1277. And that was based on the work of Pope Innocent III (1198 to 1216).[5]

The lectionary of biblical readings imposed along with the missal of Pius V went back even further. It was borrowed from the Benedictine Abbey of Murbach in the Vosges region of France. Dom Wilmart, O.S.B., has identified it as "a lectionary from the end of the eighth century" — a product of the Carolingian reform. Father Nocent, another Benedictine, says it was a fairly poor lectionary. In Advent, for example, this lectionary repeated the same reading every day of the week.[6] If we compare that with the rich ensemble of readings offered today for the season of Advent, there is little cause for regret over losing that kind of antiquity.

In the area of rubrics, John Burchard, a canon from Strasbourg, had decided the order of pontifical ceremonies in the year 1512. Using Burchard's work, the commission of Pius V retained all the gestures of the Gothic Mass — the signs of the cross, the genuflexions, the bows, and so on.

The commission did not dare break with the unusual wording of certain prayers. For example, they kept the expression "immaculate host" which was used from the Offertory on, as if the host had already been consecrated. On the other hand, they kept the signs of the cross over the host and chalice at the end of the Canon, as if the bread and wine had not already been consecrated.[7]

In the same vein, they retained the medieval approach at Communion. "The ritual of the Communion of the faithful is presented as a patching in of the Communion of the sick, introduced into the celebration of the Mass."[8] The Communion of the sick featured the *Confiteor* and two absolutions, anomalies that some dioceses had avoided and protested against.

In other words, Jungmann's appraisal, published in 1949, seems in no way extreme. He says: "So much in the Mass book and in the Mass ordo remained unaltered and perhaps even unexamined — much that during the Franco-German period had been overlaid inartistically upon the austere form of the Mass of the city of Rome, or that had during the Gothic period found a place in the Mass books *secundum usum Romanae Curiae.*"[9]

If we add what was overlooked in the missal, we are struck by "the absolute neglect of the assembly, the priest seeming to celebrate alone before these others."[10] We are forced to the conclusion that organization, unity, and orthodoxy were bought at a heavy price.

Today, with four centuries of experience behind us, even a liturgist as knowledgeable as Jungmann finds it difficult to assess the "freezing" brought about by the reform. He says that "it is hard to say whether in the period to follow, this circumstance was good fortune or bad. What would have happened to the Roman liturgy if the various irenic tendencies had taken a path of development closer to that trodden by Protestant worship? Or if the creative spirit of the Baroque had been allowed to tamper with the rite of the Mass as fully as did the Middle Ages, handling it according to its own conception of sacrament, sacrifice and solemnity?"[11]

Jungmann does not venture to answer these questions and neither do we. One's opinion is bound to be colored by fear or boldness. But let us not foist everything off on divine Providence. Christ confided his Eucharist to the free responsibility of his disciples, his Church.

In the light of the evidence, it is not unfair to say that at the time of the Council of Trent, all that the Church could offer the dawning new age was "the Autumn Mass."

Notes

1. Josef A. Jungmann, S.J., *The Mass of the Roman Rite,* Volume One, page 133.
2. Jungmann, Volume One, page 135; A.-G. Martimort, ed., *The Church at Prayer, Volume 2: The Eucharist,* page 52.
3. Jungmann, Volume One, page 138.
4. Adrien Nocent, O.S.B., *La célébration eucharistique avant et après saint Pie V,* éd. Beauchesne, Paris 1977, page 44.
5. See number 7 in the preface to the 1978 edition of the current Roman Missal.
6. Nocent, pages 45 and 52.
7. Nocent, page 51.
8. Nocent, page 52.
9. Jungmann, Volume One, page 137.
10. Nocent, page 52.
11. Jungmann, Volume One, pages 141-142.

8
From the Council of Trent to Vatican II

"Let no one change a thing!" — that was the ironclad command that accompanied the promulgation of Pius V's missal. Under such an airtight prohibition, how could there be any change during the time between Trent and Vatican II that is worth mentioning? As Jungmann notes, " . . . the missal of Pius V was indeed a powerful dam holding back the waters or permitting them to flow through only in firm, well-built canals. At one blow all arbitrary meandering to one side or another was cut off, all floods prevented . . . ."[1]

That is an arresting image, but let us look at the facts.

How the Mass of Pius V Was Received

At first the Mass of Saint Pius V received a better welcome than one might have expected. It was adopted even by dioceses whose liturgy dated back more than 200 years and were therefore exempt from it. It was also accepted by dioceses that could have avoided it by taking shelter behind royal or imperial authority.

What accounts for such a favorable reception? The following points go a long way toward explaining it.

• There was a felt need on the part of the entire Catholic community to close ranks around the pope in reaction to the Protestant separation with its already visible divisions and further splintering.

• The printed text offered convenience, even from an economic viewpoint. It was much less costly for a diocese to buy many copies of an edited missal than to edit its own.

• Finally, this text was based on the Franco-Roman and Germano-Roman Mass. It was permeated with both Roman and northern cultures. And right up to the end, it retained its Gothic coloration.

Historians find it hard to cite any opposition. Of course, there always has to be one exception, and in this case it was the diocese of Rouen in France. "In 1623, Archbishop Francois de Harlay decided to adopt the missal of Pius V. There was such opposition from the faithful that he had to reinstate the ancient observance of Rouen."[2]

We might also note that historians have always wondered whether Pius V himself ever used his own missal. Being a Dominican as well as pope, it was perfectly within bounds for him to celebrate Mass according to the Dominican liturgy.

The Dam Was Constantly Reinforced

After the reform of Pius V, along came the energetic Sixtus V, who was pope from 1585 to 1590. This pope tried to put order into everything, everywhere. He tracked down villains . . . and any fanciful straying from the straight and narrow. He reorganized the Roman Curia. He set the number of cardinals at seventy — and so it remained until Pope John XXIII added more cardinals in 1959.

On January 22, 1588, Sixtus V installed a special department of the Curia, the Congregation of Rites and Ceremonies. Presided over by five cardinals, this Congregation was to "see to it that the old sacred rites are exactly observed in all places and by all persons, in the churches of Rome and of the universe, including our pontifical chapel, in everything concerning the Mass, the Divine Office, the administration of the sacraments and, in general, other functions related to worship."

To appreciate the importance attached to this new institution, it suffices to examine the papal arrangements:

• Sixtus V put at the head of this Congregation not one but five cardinals.

• Its program was the past; it was to watch over "the old rites."

• Its jurisdiction included all places and persons that had anything to do with liturgy, especially the Mass.

• The Congregation grew and grew as special commissions were added on. As recently as February 6, 1930, Pope Pius XI added a history section to it.

This Congregation of Rites strongly reinforced Roman centralization in matters liturgical. "Until this period," writes A. Bride, "individual churches retained a certain liberty in matters of cult and ceremony; except in difficult cases, bishops and provincial councils lost practically all control."[3]

Continuing his image of the dam that "prevented all floods," Jungmann notes this sad result: ". . . the beautiful river valley now lay barren and the forces of further evolution were often channeled into the narrow bed of a very inadequate devotional life instead of gathering strength for new forms of liturgical expression."[4] Let us take a look at what this means.

The Experts at Rubrics

After Sixtus V's Congregation of Rites came on the scene as the watchdog of Pius V's liturgical legislation, there was not much for the liturgists to do. They faded out of the picture and the rubricians moved in.

These rubrical experts kept themselves busy. They anticipated possible deviations from the law. They cleared up doubts. They refined hypotheses. The rubricians gloried in their work, arguing fine points and writing volumes on issues such as the shape of the tabernacle or the length of the altar cloth. They wrote thousands of questions on such matters to Rome. Often enough, Rome's exasperated reply would be: "The question has already been asked and answered a number of times."

The emperor of Austria, Joseph II, even got into the act. With perfect seriousness, he legislated on the number of Masses to be said for such and such an intention, the days on which Benediction of the Blessed Sacrament may be celebrated, and the number of candles to be lit for a high Mass.

Frederick II, the king of Prussia, caustically called him "my brother the sacristan."

To show how far things went, here is one example among thousands chosen at random from the ceremonial for a deacon:

"When the deacon, even though he be a canon" (the Congregation of Rites felt it had to be that specific in 1827) "presents something, for example the paten or the chalice, to the celebrant, clothed in his vestments, he first kisses the object, then the hand of the celebrant; and when he receives something from him, he first kisses his hand and then the object. This rule is abrogated in Masses for the dead, in which all kissing is omitted.

"When he has the incense blessed, he receives the incense boat first with his right hand and, transferring it to his left hand, with his right hand he presents to the celebrant the spoon, which he kisses at the end which the celebrant will take, and then kisses the celebrant's hand." (Anyone who has done this knows how fast he has to move.) "Bowing his head, he says, *Benedicite, pater reverende;* then, having received the spoon with the ordinary kisses, he returns the incense boat with the spoon in it, to the thurifer" etc., etc.[5]

They did not leave out a thing.

But Meanwhile . . .

In the meantime, there was another group plodding away at research on old liturgical texts. Among them were Mabillon and his Benedictine confreres. Silently but effectively, they were laying the foundation for a true and solid liturgical renewal.

Also deserving mention is the French school of spirituality that gathered around the priests of the Oratory. At the Oratory, "worship was established from the start as the center of piety. Private prayer was deliberately allied to public liturgy. In fact, participation in the oblation of Christ gradually became the fundamental concept of piety in the school of Berulle, of Condren (d. 1641), and of Olier (d.

1657). Thus in regard to the Mass, the sacrifice of the Church and with it the liturgical side of the sacrifice became more prominent."[6]

In 1690, Father Pierre LeBrun of the Oratory taught courses in liturgy at Saint-Magloire in Paris. From his lectures, which were very popular, he developed a masterly work in four volumes entitled *The Literal, Historical, and Dogmatic Explanation of the Prayers and Ceremonies of the Mass,* published in Paris between the years 1716 and 1726. Volume One explains the prayers of the Latin Mass, making frequent reference to medieval variants which are often the only key to understanding the prayers. Volumes Two and Three study other ancient liturgies of the East and West, and Volume Four is about Protestant forms of worship. The four volumes were reprinted many times during the eighteenth century. According to M. Join-Lambert, LeBrun's "monument of erudition remained unsurpassed until the appearance of the contemporary liturgical work and studies of Father Jungmann."[7]

It was not until the end of the nineteenth century and the beginning of the twentieth that any truly satisfactory discoveries, critical editions, and studies appeared in the area of liturgy. But it would be unfair to overlook or minimize the work of those who painstakingly prepared the way.

Latin — the Main Buttress of the Dam

Between the Council of Trent and Vatican II, Latin played a role in the evolution of the liturgy, pushing the logic of uniformity to the absurd. Its story deserves to be told, if only as an example.

The pros and cons of using different languages in the Mass had been discussed at the Council of Trent and the conclusion reached was this: *"If anyone shall say . . . that the Mass ought to be celebrated in the vernacular tongue only . . . let him be anathema."*[8]

The Council's position was nuanced. It left the door open to a limited use of the vernacular. But by forbidding any change at all in his missal, Pius V implicitly closed the door to any language but Latin. His successors reinforced that prohibition, as the following incident shows. "Apparently fearing that an effort was being made to introduce the vernacular into the Mass, Alexander VII had in 1661 condemned a translation of the Roman Missal into French and had forbidden any further translations under pain of excommunication."[9]

On September 1, 1759, an even stronger directive went out to missionaries in China. It made clear that "the prayers to be said in the vernacular by the people at Mass were not to be those said by celebrant or deacon or altar boy *(servente)* or choir."[10]

As time went on, Rome continued to insist that the prayers of the Mass not be brought within people's reach. In 1857, Pius IX renewed the prohibition. It was not until 1898 that translations of the missal were no longer censured and put on the Index of Prohibited Books.[11]

Water Flows Around the Dam

Little by little, preaching became separated from the Mass. It was either done before Mass or at some other time. When it did take place during the Mass, it rarely had any connection to the Gospel of the day. Also, in those days, a custom remaining from the Middle Ages dictated that the pulpit be located far from the altar.

The people generally received Communion after Mass. But they did not receive after the parish high Mass because the law of fasting induced people to receive after earlier Masses, which were usually low Masses. As a result, Communion was separated from the Mass, and people considered it more a sharing in the Real Presence than a taking part in the sacrifice of the Mass.[12] Also, at that time, the religious attitude called Jansenism was influencing people to receive Communion even less often than before.

The prayer book became one of the means people used to occupy themselves during Mass. In the prayer books there was a lopsided emphasis on individual piety and no emphasis on community participation. Another thing about prayer books was that only the educated could make use of them.

Most people were unable to use prayer books, so they were taught songs and prayers for group use by the Jesuits and others who gave parish missions. In Germany, Saint Peter Canisius — a Jesuit — tirelessly preached and taught church songs in German.[13] At Mass people also recited the rosary aloud, aided sometimes by a commentary.

Chant and Music

From the end of the Middle Ages on, stress was put on the development of musical accompaniment. This emphasis was even greater after the Council of Trent. "Encouraged by the moderate attitude of the Council of Trent, it had developed into mighty proportions. . . . Besides the organ, there were accompaniments by other instruments."

But unfortunately, this music forgot its original purpose, which was to accompany the Mass. "As a result of this, the music often fitted very poorly into the liturgical setting. And since this latter was but little understood, and because esthetic consideration began to hold sway, the liturgy was not only submerged under this ever-growing art but actually suppressed."[14] Celebrations on great feasts were like concerts in church. While the choir kept on singing the *Credo,* the priest would go on with the Offertory. The priest himself sang only the opening lines of the Preface and the *Pater noster.*

It was during this period that the choir left the sanctuary and moved to the choir loft where the organ had already relocated.[15] The *Kyrie, Sanctus,* and *Agnus Dei* in several voices added splendor to great feasts and fed the pride of triumphant choirmasters.

However, people like the Germans, blessed with strong singing voices, were not about to let themselves be left out by a choir. In the eighteenth century "no one had any misgivings about combining the new *Singmesse* with a chanted Mass as well as with a low Mass."[16] And so the German sung Mass was born. It was used throughout the nineteenth century and finally approved by Rome on December 24, 1943.[17]

To a purist, the term *sung Mass* sounds odd. Is it really the Mass that is sung? "As a matter of fact the German *Singmesse* . . . gave somewhat the impression of a one-sided conversation, for not only the orations but the readings (or at least the Epistle) and the preface and *Pater noster,* none of them unimportant parts in the structure of the Mass, do not receive any kind of expression."[18]

All this singing, all these ways people had of keeping themselves occupied, were legal. They did not violate the obligation to use Latin, which the priest was doing. Latin did not bother people in the least; they could do something else and do it in their own language.

Official Changes in the Missal

Strong as it was, the dam eventually buckled. There had, in fact, been concessions to Pius V's interdictions right from the start, all made very officially in conformity with the law.

As far back as 1604, less than fifty years after publication, Pope Clement VIII declared that many printing errors had crept into the edited missals. He added that certain translations of the Bible used in the missal of Pius V needed improvement. Rubrics, too, needed to be presented more clearly. So he introduced these improvements into the unalterable Roman Missal. In 1634, Pope Urban VIII also revised certain hymns in the missal.

Another kind of official change took place with the introduction of new Masses and texts. In the eighteenth century the Preface of the Blessed Trinity was prescribed by Pope Clement XIII for Sunday Masses. Nearer to our day, Pope Leo XIII imposed prayers after Mass, which became the obligatory way of concluding the Mass.

More important reforms took place in the twentieth century: Saint Pius X's changes regarding Holy Communion, and Pope Pius XII's changes in the Office for Holy Week. Then, finally convinced that the rubrics of Saint Pius V were no longer appropriate, Pope John XXIII on July 23, 1960 — the eve of the Second Vatican Council — promulgated a whole new set of rubrics for the Mass.[19]

These are not exciting details, but they point up an important fact: popes have never thought that Pius V's decision took away their right to modify the missal he imposed.

Opposition to Pope Pius V

In spite of Pius V's closed-door policy, other missals besides his were composed, printed, and used more or less officially in various places. "By 1791" — in France alone — "eighty French dioceses had abandoned the Roman liturgy, and uniformity of the official prayer was nothing more than a memory."[20]

In 1801 Pope Pius VII signed a concordat with Napoleon, who ruled France. The concordat changed the boundary lines of French dioceses and, in its wake, only twelve dioceses in all of France ended up following the Roman liturgy. In some dioceses there were four, seven, and sometimes as many as nine missals in use — for example, at Versailles and Beauvais. The liturgy was in chaos.[21]

The same was true of the breviary, the book of daily psalms and prayers used by priests and monks. As far back as 1568, Pius V had reformed the breviary and imposed it with the same conditions as the missal. In 1798, 900 priests were grouped together on the prison ships of Rochefort. These priest-martyrs had only a few breviaries, all of them different. The priests found it impossible to pray the breviary in common.[22]

In fairness to the liturgical lawbreakers, we must realize that the mentality of that era was far different from our own. For ages the prevailing assumption had been that new Mass texts could be composed, without special authorization, whenever the needs of a diocese or religious order required it.[23]

The Return of the Mass of Pius V — 1833 to 1860

After the French Revolution, there was a gradual return to Roman unity. This was largely due to the works of the Benedictine abbot Dom Guéranger (1807 to 1875), who succeeded in getting the missal of Saint Pius V adopted without the least modification. "The struggle for the Roman liturgy of Saint Pius V ended around the middle of the (nineteenth) century with complete victory for its proponents. Too complete, we might even say, and Dom Guéranger was not the last to regret it. For, most of the time, the faithful let themselves be satisfied with unquestioning acceptance of the Roman liturgy. They gave no thought to salvaging Gallican prayers and observances of respectable antiquity that Rome would surely have approved."[24]

Abbé Jacquemet, citing Pierre Paris, gives the same assessment: "The movement actually surpassed the limits set by its promoter, Dom Guéranger. At the risk of bewildering the simple in their devotions, they sacrificed customs grown dear to them, inherited from time immemorial. They abandoned observances which were among the most authentic of Roman antiquity, to which France alone had remained obstinately faithful. These regrettable exaggerations, mingled with a liturgical restoration both necessary and opportune to which the name of Dom Guéranger will always be attached, are certainly no cause for rejoicing."[25]

The Benedictine abbey of Solemnes in France played a role in that success. Under the leadership of abbots Poithier, Mocquereau, and Gajard, Solemnes restored Gregorian chant, which had great influence on the restoration of the Roman liturgy.

The mid-twentieth century ended that period by launching a new reform, one which stood a better chance of surviving insofar as it was grounded in solid preparation. But twenty centuries of history filled with contrasting elements left the

Church with a difficult choice between two options. One option was the principle of Saint Callistus: to celebrate the liturgy in a living language capable of fostering intelligent participation in the sacrifice of Christ by the People of God. The other option was to indulge the dream of literal and perfect unity, an ever-recurring dream that has always ended in failure. Even the iron rigor of Saint Pius V and Sixtus V's hairsplitting Congregation of Rites were unable to bring that dream to reality.

What was the Spirit of Pentecost telling the Church, the Spirit of many tongues, the Spirit of communion and unity?

Notes

1. Josef A. Jungmann, S.J., *The Mass of the Roman Rite,* Volume One, page 140.
2. J. Gaillard, O.S.B., "Gallicane (liturgie)," in the encyclopedia *Catholicisme hier, aujourd'hui, demain,* éd. Letouzey et Ané, tome 4, Paris 1956, column 1729.
3. A. Bride, "Rite," in *Dictionnaire de Théologie Catholique,* éd. Letouzey et Ané, tome 13, Paris 1937, column 2738.
4. Jungmann, Volume One, page 141.
5. M. l'Abbé Boissonnet, *Dictionnaire des cérémonies et des rites sacrés,* in the *Encyclopédie théologique* of L'Abbé Migne, tome 15, Montrouge 1846, column 1098.
6. Jungmann, Volume One, page 143 (drawing from H. Bremond, *Histoire littéraire du Sentiment religieux en France,* volume III, Paris 1916).
7. M. Join-Lambert, *"Le Brun (Pierre),"* in the encyclopedia *Catholicisme hier, aujourd'hui, demain,* éd. Letouzey et Ané, tome 7, Paris 1975, column 142.
8. The Council of Trent, Canons on the Sacrifice of the Mass, Canon 9, Denziger 956.
9. Jungmann, Volume One, page 143.
10. Jungmann, Volume One, page 144, note 15.
11. Adrien Nocent, O.S.B., *La célébration eucharistique avant et après saint Pie V,* page 60.
12. Jungmann, Volume One, page 148.
13. Jungmann, Volume One, page 146.
14. Jungmann, Volume One, page 149.

15. Jungmann, Volume One, page 149.
16. Jungmann, Volume One, page 155.
17. Jungmann, Volume One, page 156, note 79.
18. Jungmann, Volume One, page 156.
19. Nocent, page 62.
20. J. Gaillard, op. cit., column 1730.
21. Dom Cabrol, *Liturgia,* page 872.
22. Dom Cabrol, page 87.
23. Jungmann, Volume One, page 141, note 1.
24. Dom Cabrol, page 872.
25. L'Abbé Jacquemet, "Guéranger," in the encyclopedia *Catholicisme hier, aujourd'hui, demain,* éd. Letouzey et Ané, tome 5, Paris 1962, column 326.

9
The Choice of Vatican II
and the Missal of Paul VI

This book has spoken favorably of the Vatican II reform and the missal of Pope Paul VI. This chapter, then, might be expected to launch into a paean of praise. Before we praise, let us try to understand what Vatican II opted for, and what that choice entails for the People of God.

It is important to understand this choice in the light of history. So, anyone tempted to go straight to the author's "bottom-line" assessment by reading this chapter first is advised against it. As Saint-Exupéry noted, "You reach the summit only of those slopes you have actually scaled."

In the history of the Mass, the choice of Vatican II is of millenial proportion. A person can reject that choice outright in the name of yesterday's religion, or accept it in blind faith as an absolute. Both cases rule out the use of our intelligence. The genesis of that choice provides its only explanation, and that genesis goes back far beyond the half century we are about to examine. We must go back to the Council of Trent, which is not itself easy to understand.

Prelude to Reform: Reaching Out to the People

On January 25, 1959, Pope John XXIII first mentioned his plan to convoke the Second Vatican Council. When we read the history of the half-century leading up to Vatican II, we can see that liturgical reform had become inevitable. It was already in the making, but on a totally different track from the one taken by the Council of Trent.

In 1903 Pope Saint Pius X insisted that Gregorian chant, which was in full revival, be sung by the people. In 1905, in his decree *Sacra Tridentina Synodus*, Pius X put the lid on a heated controversy by calling the faithful to frequent and even daily Communion. Then, in his 1910 decree *Quam Singulari*, Pius extended his call for frequent Communion to children who have reached the age of reason.

Meanwhile, in Belgium, Dom Lambert Beauduin gave new life to the liturgical movement inspired by Dom Guéranger. He took it from the monastery and brought it to people in parishes.

From 1920 on, the missals of Dom Lefebvre made the long-untranslated Mass prayers available to people in their own language, allowing them that degree of participation.

In Austria, Father Pius Parsch added a biblical dimension to the liturgical renewal in a way people could grasp.

In the United States, the center of liturgical renewal was the Benedictine abbey of St. John in Collegeville, Minnesota. Collegeville publishes the excellent magazine *Worship* (originally called *Orate, Fratres)* which has been at the forefront of renewal throughout the decades, including those preceding Vatican II. Liturgical scholars who were pastors, such as H. A. Reinhold and Martin Hellriegel, planted the seeds of renewal in their writings and parish liturgies.

At Maria-Laach, a monastery in Germany, Dom Odo Casel and his group studied the link between ancient liturgy and the history of religions, paving the way for restoration of the Easter liturgy.[1] Casel's work convinced Pope Pius XII; in 1951 the pope restored the ancient ceremonies of Holy Saturday night, and in 1955 all of Holy Week.

As far back as 1947, in his encyclical letter *Mediator Dei*, Pius XII encouraged dialogue Masses.[2] Following the logic of his 1943 encyclical *The Mystical Body of Christ, Mediator Dei* defined the liturgy as "the public worship . . . rendered by the Mystical Body of Christ in the entirety of its Head and members",[3] words which Vatican II adopted as its own.[4] In other words, liturgy is not only worship by Jesus Christ or by the priest acting "in the person of Christ" but worship by the entire Church united to its head. The *people* must therefore *act with* the *priest*.

The following year, 1948, Pius XII established a "commission for general liturgical reform." For awhile he even considered restoring concelebration.[5]

After the Second World War, many French people associated with the magazine *La Maison-Dieu* sparked hopes for renewal by holding congresses of pastoral liturgy and starting parish liturgy groups which became widespread.

At the opening session of the Second Vatican Council in 1962, the bishops sent back for revision a text proposed for the Constitution on the Church. Then, by an overwhelming majority, they immediately accepted the plan proposed for the Constitution on the Liturgy and began work on it. After much discussion and revision, the document was voted on by the Fathers of the Council. The final tally was 2,147 in favor, 4 against. Pope Paul VI promulgated it on December 4, 1963.

That was the end of an age. In its first paragraph, the Constitution states "several aims" of the Council, one of them being "to adapt more suitably to the needs of our times those institutions which are subject to *change*." It goes on to say that the Council "sees particularly cogent reasons for undertaking the *reform* and promotion of the liturgy." There it was: a program of liturgical *change,* the word held taboo for the missal of Pius V.

In chapters 2 through 7, the Constitution on the Liturgy speaks about the Eucharist, Sacraments and Sacramentals, the Divine Office, the Liturgical Year, Sacred Music, Sacred Art and Furnishings. Everything is to be "revised." (The documents of Vatican II were written in Latin. In the Liturgy Constitution, the Latin verb translated in English as "revise" is *recognoscere.)* The word is repeated twenty times.

The Direction of Reform: Participation

The Liturgy Constitution emphasizes the Real Presence of Christ, just as *Mediator Dei* had done.[6] But at Vatican II there was no longer a need, as there had been at Trent, to debate with Protestants over the matter. Vatican II characterizes the liturgy as "an *action of Christ* the Priest *and of His Body* which is the Church."[7] Liturgical celebration is an *action* we do with Christ.

The most famous affirmation in the Liturgy Constitution says: ". . . the liturgy is the summit toward which the activity of the Church is directed; at the same time it is the fount from which all her power flows." The rest of the statement makes it clear that the word *Church* here means all the faithful.[8] Referring to the priesthood exercised by all the faithful, another Council document, the Constitution on the Church, repeats the same formula in condensed form: "Taking part in the Eucharistic Sacrifice, which is the fount and apex of the whole Christian life, they [the faithful] offer the divine Victim to God, and offer themselves along with it." (The paragraph also points out that there are differences between the roles of priests and the rest of the faithful.)[9]

It comes as no surprise, then, that the key word in the Liturgy Constitution is *participation*. All seven chapters of the document use the word. It is repeated as a verb and as a noun twenty-six times.

Chapter 1 of the document issues a solemn call for full participation:

"Mother Church earnestly desires that all the faithful should be led to that full, conscious, and active participation in liturgical celebrations which is demanded by the very nature of the liturgy . . . this full and active participation is the aim to be considered before all else; for it is the primary and indispensable source from which the faithful are to derive the true Christian spirit . . . ." (14)

Chapter 2, on the Mystery of the Eucharist, says:

"The Church, therefore, earnestly desires that Christ's faithful, when present at this mystery of faith, should not be there as strangers or silent spectators; on the contrary, through a good understanding of the rites and prayers they should take part in the sacred action conscious of what they are doing, with devotion and full collaboration." (48)

Vatican II, then, issued a serious call for full participation in the liturgy. This is not a truth to be believed, but a program, a task to be accomplished. The quality and depth of the task go beyond changes in rubrics.

The Risks of Reform

According to the principle of Saint Callistus, participation by the assembly logically calls for use of living languages in the liturgy. Vatican II, however, began with only a cautious move toward vernacular languages. Article 36 in the Liturgy Constitution, for example, says that Latin is to be observed in the Latin rites but that "the mother tongue" may be of greater advantage to the people and "the limits of its employment may be extended."

But chapter 2 on the Eucharist reverses the roles of Latin and the mother tongue. Article 54 says that the readings and the Prayer of the Faithful may be in the mother tongue, but that people should *also* — in Latin, *etiam* — be able to say or sing their parts in Latin. So here, Latin is not the basic norm but is the language people should *also* be able to use.

The third-century quarrel between Greek and Latin — Hippolytus and Callistus — comes to mind. If we side with Callistus and say that people should understand what they are praying, what happens to the principle of unity that started with Charlemagne and continued with the missal of Pius V? Catholics in the world today speak over 300 languages.[10] Did Vatican II realize the amount of diversity it was letting itself in for? Good-bye now, any thought of one missal for all.

As a matter of fact, Vatican II did think of that. In line with the options of missionaries in its Decree on the Missions, the Liturgy Constitution states:

"Even in the liturgy, the Church has no wish to impose a rigid uniformity in matters which do not implicate the faith or the good of the whole community; rather does she respect and foster the genius and talents of the various races and peoples. Anything in these peoples' way of life which is not indissolubly bound up with superstition and error she studies with sympathy and, if possible, preserves intact. Sometimes in fact she admits such things into the liturgy itself, so long as they harmonize with its true and authentic spirit.'' (37)

But doesn't that open the door to the kind of fanciful innovations that in the past have led to liturgical anarchy?

To avoid that outcome, careful safeguards were put in place:

• ''Regulation of the sacred liturgy depends solely on the authority of the Church, that is, on the Apostolic See and, as laws may determine, on the bishop'' — and on ''various kinds of competent territorial bodies of bishops legitimately established.'' (22, #1 and #2) Regulation of the liturgy does not, therefore, belong to one bishop claiming the right to celebrate according to an ancient rite, however venerable, which Rome no longer upholds.

• Liturgical adaptation is not left up to the whim of this or that priest acting on his own. The Liturgy Constitution states: ''Therefore no other person, even if he be a priest, may add, remove, or change anything in the liturgy on his own authority.'' (22, #3)

Of course, when the liturgy offers a number of options to choose from, or invites the celebrant to formulate his own intentions, or authorizes him to experiment, that is a different matter. Article 40 states:

''In some places and circumstances, however, an even more radical adaptation of the liturgy is needed, and this entails greater difficulties. Wherefore. . . .'' It then goes on to say that (a) the competent authority must consider which elements from the traditions of individual peoples might be admitted into divine worship and submit them to the Apostolic See, by whose consent they may be introduced, and (b) the Apostolic See will grant power to the authority to permit and to direct the experiments.

Everything is to be reviewed. Everything is to be reworked.

As Father Dominique Dye has commented, ''Although several historians disagree with this characterization, we might compare the conciliar Constitution to a legal framework. The Council has issued a work charter calling the Apostolic See, episcopal conferences, priests, lay people, and specialists to a work of remodeling."[11]

The Council of Trent left it up to the pope to flesh out the liturgical reform it called for. In its turn, Vatican II was content to sketch only the broad outlines of the task ahead. The Liturgy Constitution foresaw a new choice of texts from Holy Scripture (article 51), the restoration of the homily (article 52) and of the Prayer of the Faithful (article 53), of Communion under both species (article 55), and of concelebration (articles 57 and 58). It also foresaw the revision of the liturgical year (article 107). The truth is, it called for a rebuilding of the whole liturgical edifice.

The Missal of Paul VI — Haste and Prudence

As early as 1964 — before the close of the Council in December 1965 — Pope Paul VI set up a commission composed of fifty cardinals and bishops from all parts of the world. This commission supervised the work of an international group of liturgical experts which included pastors of parishes.

The working group was first rank. Among its members were Johannes Wagner, director of the Liturgical Institute in Trier, Germany; (the shortly thereafter named Bishop) Hänggi of Basle, Switzerland; the renowned Austrian liturgist Josef Jungmann (from whose *Mass of the Roman Rite* this book so often quotes); Roman professor Cyprian Vagaggini, and Fathers Gy and Jounel from France. In 1966 this group was joined by the French Fathers Bouyer and Gélineau and Dom Bernard Botte of Louvain.

On May 23, 1967, Paul VI authorized new Eucharistic Prayers, which were the core project of the working group. The pope allowed a full year for reactions and reflection. Then, on Holy Thursday, April 3, 1969, he promulgated the Constitution, *Missale Romanum*. The new Roman Missal appeared on March 26, 1970, and a revised edition with minor changes came out on Holy Thursday, 1975. Most of the translations into Western languages took four years — until 1974. The whole missal project lasted ten years, from 1964 to 1974.

That seemed a long time to priests who were anxious to put the Council's options into practice. But it is hard to see how the commission could have worked any faster. And we might have to concede a point made by Dom Nocent. He noted: "If one can raise any objection to what was done, it would have to be at the level of preparing the people. This was not done, it seems, for a long enough time before the liturgical changes took place."[12]

Experts were polishing their work, bishops were issuing directives, the pope was pondering, and translators were sharpening their pencils. Everybody involved was thinking in terms of history: the days of old, yesterday, today, and tomorrow. But meanwhile, what about preparing the people for changes that would shatter a liturgical mold that was centuries old?

The Missal of Paul VI — Unity and Diversity

"The most remarkable of the new features are those which concern the great Eucharistic Prayer" — the very heart of the Mass. That is how Pope Paul VI expressed it in *Missale Romanum,* the Apostolic Constitution of April 3, 1969.[13]

Let them remodel the opening part of the Mass with a new penitential rite. Let them simplify the Offertory. Let them highlight the final blessing by suppressing the Last Gospel. Fine. But touch the *Canon*?

Pope Paul VI gave a good explanation why he had touched the Canon:

"In the Roman rite the first part of this prayer, known as the Preface, has indeed acquired many different texts in the course of the centuries; but the second part, known as the Canon, assumed an unchanging form about the fourth or fifth century. By contrast, the oriental liturgies have ever admitted a certain variety in their anaphoras (prayers expressing the sacrificial offering).

"Besides enriching the Eucharistic Prayer by providing a larger selection of Prefaces" — there were twenty Prefaces in the missal at the time of Pope John XXIII; today there are over eighty — "(some drawn from the more ancient traditions of the Roman Church and some newly composed) *we have decided now to add three more Canons (anaphoras) for use in that prayer.*"[14]

The First Eucharistic Prayer

Of prime importance is the fact that the missal of Paul VI kept the very venerable Roman Canon — the Canon that goes back not only to Saint Pius V but to Saint Ambrose in the fourth century.

Only three slight changes were made in it:

— The first change consists of the added words *"which will be given up for you"* after "this is my body" at the consecration of the bread.

— The second change is the new wording *"Do this in memory of me"* after the consecration of the cup. (The old wording, which was in Latin, said: "As often as you do this, you shall do it in my memory.")

— The third change is the celebrant's line, *"Let us proclaim the mystery of faith"* (after the consecration of the chalice) to which all respond, "Christ has died," etc. or one of the other optional responses.

These changes were made in order to establish a certain amount of unity among the four Eucharistic Prayers. *All four use this same formula.*

As Pope Paul explained, ". . . for pastoral reasons, and so as to facilitate concelebration, we have ordered that the words of our Lord shall be the same in all forms of the Canon. In every Eucharistic Prayer, therefore, we wish these words to be as follows:

Over the bread:

'TAKE THIS, ALL OF YOU, AND EAT IT;
THIS IS MY BODY WHICH WILL BE GIVEN UP FOR YOU.'

Over the wine:
'TAKE THIS, ALL OF YOU, AND DRINK FROM IT;
THIS IS THE CUP OF MY BLOOD,
THE BLOOD OF THE NEW AND EVERLASTING
COVENANT.
IT WILL BE SHED FOR YOU AND FOR ALL MEN
SO THAT SINS MAY BE FORGIVEN.
DO THIS IN MEMORY OF ME.' ''

(In Canada and the United States, the word *men* in the phrase "for all men" was subsequently deleted from the institution narrative in all approved Eucharistic Prayers. For the United States, this permission from the pope was granted in a letter dated November 17, 1981, from the Apostolic Delegate, Archbishop Pio Laghi, to the National Conference of Catholic Bishops. For Canada, the same permission was granted in a letter dated March 10, 1982, from Archbishop Giuseppe Casoria, Pro-Prefect of the Sacred Congregation for the Sacraments and Divine Worship, to Archbishop Henri Legaré, President of the Canadian Conference of Catholic Bishops. This modification was allowed for pastoral reasons in response to concerns about the use of sexist language in the prayer of the Church, *ed.*)

The pope went on to say:

"The words, 'The mystery of faith,' spoken by the priest are to be taken out of the context of the words spoken by our Lord, and used instead to introduce an acclamation by the faithful."[15]

If you compare this wording with the words of Paul, Luke, Mark, and Matthew near the end of the Foundation Chapter in this book, you have to agree that the wording of Paul VI echoes primitive tradition. No one who recalls the conclusion of our Foundation Chapter could quarrel with these changes.

The Second Eucharistic Prayer

With this second Eucharistic Prayer, Pope Paul VI gave us a Canon that is even more ancient than the venerable Eucharistic Prayer I from the fourth century. If you turn back to chapter 2, "The Mass in the Time of the Persecutions," you can compare Eucharistic Prayer II with the one given there (pages 38-39). The parallels are obvious.

Cardinal Hoeffner of Cologne, Germany, put it well when he said: "The second prayer, which takes us back to the time of the martyrs, is both vigorous and clear."[16]

The bishops in northern France declared: "It yields its admirable riches to the reader with solid biblical and theological background."[17]

And Monsignor Martimort, author and editor of the well-known *The Church at Prayer,* identifies it for us. "It is," he says, "that of Hippolytus of Rome, at the beginning of the third century."[18]

It is short and meaningful, well-suited to the simplicity of daily Masses.

The Third Eucharistic Prayer

Eucharistic Prayer III owes its beginning to Dom Cyprian Vagaggini, professor of liturgy at the Roman Institute, Regina Mundi. This Canon is rich with overtones of Alexandrian, Byzantine, and Maronite anaphoras. According to Jounel, it even contains "a borrowing from Gallican liturgy."[19]

This Eucharistic Prayer expresses the doctrine of the Eucharistic sacrifice in an especially clear way. It says: "Look with favor on your Church's offering, and see the Victim whose death has reconciled us to yourself." That is an excellent statement of the Church's sacrifice in its relation to the unique sacrifice of Christ.

In addition, this third prayer gives rightful prominence to the Holy Spirit. It names the Spirit four times, which helps to temper the amazement of our Eastern-rite brethren over the fact that our Canon made no mention of the Holy Spirit except in the doxology.

This prayer, like Eucharistic Prayer I, is well adapted to the solemnity of a Sunday gathering.

The Fourth Eucharistic Prayer

Eucharistic Prayer IV borrows from the Eastern liturgy, especially the Greek. But it goes back even farther, to the liturgy of the synagogue and of Jewish meals which gave birth to the first Christian prayers.

In this prayer we praise God for his many wonders and sing our hope of deliverance. It is a profoundly biblical prayer which recounts the great moments in salvation history and links our own history to its center — Christ. This Canon is excellent for use on days of recollection and on solemn feasts.

All four Eucharistic Prayers are a rich source of Christian faith. As Cardinal Hoeffner remarked, "Whoever consciously opens himself to the profundity of thought in these Eucharistic Prayers must necessarily be enriched by them."[20]

New Texts, New Options

The new missal deserves credit for the wealth of new biblical readings it offers. The Sunday readings for Advent, Lent, and Easter reveal the oft-contrasted parallel between the Old and New Testaments. The first reading gives the Old Testament figure and the third reading — the Gospel — gives the New Testament fulfillment.

The second reading, the Epistle, is supposed to have continuity with the other two. The truth is, it harmonizes poorly with them. (Further revision seems to be needed here. Some of these readings would fit better after Communion, as an echo of what was proclaimed earlier.)

In the new missal the liturgical year has a good balance between "temporal" Masses centered on Christ and "sanctoral" Masses commemorating saints. Through the ages, Masses for saints have tended to dominate — an example of how "devotions" risk supplanting *the* devotion and faith itself.

A little-appreciated strength of the new missal lies in the many votive Mass options it offers for varying situations.

According to Pope Paul VI, particular care was given to the prayers. Their number was greatly increased. Some are from ancient liturgical sources, others are new to meet new needs. For example, each day of Advent, Christmastide, Lent, and Eastertide has its own prayers.

A Controlled Variety

Saint Pius V presented his missal to the Christian people "as an instrument of liturgical unity." Paul VI hoped that his new missal would help people to "witness to each other and strengthen the one faith common to all, since it enables one and the same prayer, expressed in so many different languages, to ascend to the heavenly Father through our High Priest Jesus Christ in the Holy Spirit. . . ."[21]

The "many different languages" in no way exclude Latin; the original of the new *Missale Romanum* is in Latin and may be used just as it is. But the ancient missal of Saint Pius V is excluded. It may be used only with special permission, by priests unable to adapt to the new missal and celebrating in private, with no participation by the people.

This exclusion caused a predictable stir. After all, the missal of Pius V enjoyed a virtual monopoly for four centuries. The difficulty seems to stem from the fact that its exclusion was ordered by the very pope, Paul VI, who was restoring variety.

The reform of Vatican II and Paul VI carries us back beyond the days of apparent uniformity to the early centuries of Christianity. But there is a difference in direction. The spontaneous, improvised liturgies of early Christianity moved toward unity under Charlemagne and into a state of fixed uniformity under Saint Pius V. Today we have left that uniformity behind and moved in the opposite direction toward variety, cultural diversity, and a certain degree of spontaneity. On the path of reform, there is a controlled variety that allows practically all liturgical forms. It is the exclusion of that one form — the missal of Pius V — that vexes some people.

Some people feel that the old liturgy could have been kept for at least a time. Even among those who welcomed the new Mass, some would like to go back once in awhile to the liturgical style of their childhood. Others object that this would spark conflict between parishes. In the end, it may all come down to the attraction of forbidden fruit. Even under Pope Pius XII, many already agreed that the liturgy was out of date. Stripped of its forbidden status, would the old liturgy retain its staunch followers? Who knows?

In actual fact, the Mass of Pius V has not been banned. Its heart, the Canon — in Latin, if one wishes — remains intact in the first Eucharistic Prayer of the new missal. But Pope Paul VI knew from experience that half-measures are worse than no measures at all. So he put his own reform in place, implementing Vatican II, with the same vigor that Pius V used in promoting his reform, implementing the Council of Trent.

The new missal was well received by the great majority of Christians. No sensible person any longer believes that the solution would be to turn back to the texts and rites in the missal of Pius V. Anyone who is not convinced can compare the riches of the new missal with the narrowness and poverty of the old — especially its ban against living languages, now that there are so many young Churches around the world.

The real problems of the future lie at a deeper level.

In the Language of the People

Vatican II opened the door fairly wide to vernacular languages. As we saw, this did not rule out Latin. The only stipulation was that Latin Masses be celebrated with the missal of Paul VI.

Masses in Latin with participation by the people are celebrated in various places. At St. Matthew's Cathedral in Washington, D.C., for example, there is a Latin Mass each Sunday from September through June. At these Masses, the Liturgy of the Word and other parts are in English, but the Eucharistic Prayer is entirely in Latin. In most places around the world, however, the Mass is celebrated in the more than 300 languages spoken by Catholics.

"Latin is lost. And there goes Gregorian chant along with it. The beautiful unity of being able to attend Mass in the same way everywhere is destroyed." That was the lament heard from some tourists going to Sunday Mass at churches in Spain or Italy or Japan. Their complaint was that they could not take part in the singing. (All of a sudden, people who hardly sang a note at Mass in their home parishes found their vocal cords.) But why should Catholics in Spain or Japan give up their own language just for tourists? You might think tourists could enter into the spirit of singing whose meaning was no more obscure to them than the meaning of Latin hymns. They might even have thought to delight in the fact that the languages of these foreign lands were being used to celebrate the glory of our one Catholic faith.

It is true that most Gregorian chants are no longer used at our Eucharists. The nostalgia for lost treasure is all the greater because new hymns and chants seldom achieve the artistic maturity of the ancient melodies. On this point, Dom Nocent made a realistic comment: "We cannot expect to catch up in fifteen years to what seven centuries brought to Gregorian chant."[22] Gregorian chant took seven centuries of continuous creation. Its masterpieces spread only gradually from monastery to monastery. And we ended up with only the pearls.

Today, in every land, new canticles are being born. In time some of them will attain the glory of a *Te Deum* or an *Exultet*. An immense task lies ahead.

In the Culture of the People

One of the major convictions of the Second Vatican Council is that the Good News of salvation transcends "every particularity of race or nation and therefore cannot be considered foreign anywhere or to anybody."[23]

About young Churches in the world, the Council declared: "From the customs and traditions of their people, from their wisdom and their learning, from their arts and sciences, these Churches borrow all those things which can contribute to the glory of their Creator, the revelation of the Savior's grace, or the proper arrangement of Christian life."[24]

The culture of each country creates the liturgical environment: church architecture, the style of vestments, of music, of liturgical gestures, of penance, praise, and adoration, right into the heart of the Mystery. So — if language is the central mirror of every culture — how can literary creations be the sole exception?

Here is where the obligation to use a single missal, translated from Latin, poses a problem. A translation, however excellent, of a masterpiece from an ancient language brings out only the flavor of that ancient culture. This is true of the Psalms and of the entire Bible. A prayer from Saint Leo the Great can help me to appreciate the conciseness of uncluttered Latin; I might even be inspired to compose new prayers along the same lines. But am I really involving my own cultural background in the Eucharistic memorial?

Expressions in Eucharistic Prayer I, such as "your altar in heaven" and "your angel may take this sacrifice," are puzzling no matter what language they are in. Such cases have to be what prompted Pope Paul VI to call for new prayers that are in touch with the minds of the living as well as in touch with ancient sources.

Dom Rouillard saw the problem clearly: "English literature, translated into French, remains English literature. The same holds true for the whole of the Roman liturgy. Experience confirms the fact that the use of a living language implies the difficult but indispensable creation of texts composed directly in that language, conformed to contemporary mentality. Otherwise, the liturgy, even when translated, is in danger of remaining in a foreign language."[25]

Must the cultural expression of a people in the liturgy be confined to hymns, homilies, and Prayers of the Faithful? Must a people's culture be excluded from the missal because its texts can only be translations?

Perhaps we have seen enough here to understand, if not to excuse, the cropping up of unauthorized liturgical texts — "Eucharistic Prayers" for marriages, funerals, and so on — which have had to be denounced many times. The official condemnation reads: ". . . some individuals, acting on private initiative, arrived at hasty and sometimes unwise solutions, and made changes, additions or simplifications which at times went against the basic principles of the liturgy. This only troubled the faithful and impeded or made more difficult the progress of genuine renewal."[26] Private denunciations have been no less eloquent; unauthorized texts have been called affectations, platitudes, in-group formulas, and so on.

Despite the condemnations, the phenomenon points to a valid request poorly heard. A good number of the Sunday prayers, for example, hardly interpret the sensibilities and vision people have of God's designs today.

Missals contain a Proper for nations and dioceses — Masses in honor of this or that saint. Couldn't the Holy See empower episcopal conferences to integrate prayers — even Eucharistic Prayers — into the missal of each cultural area? This could be an authentic product of an encounter between Tradition (known by experts) and their culture (known by their poets). Episcopal conferences have already allowed Eucharistic Prayers for Children and a Eucharistic Prayer for Reconciliation.

We must say No to anarchy, but Yes to the Church implanting its liturgy in each culture, according to the spirit of the Council and the spirit of Pentecost. The most delicate of tasks awaits us.

Liturgy into Life, or Life into Mystery?

The major question about vernacular liturgies goes still deeper.

"The joys and the hopes, the griefs and the anxieties of the men of this age, especially those who are poor or in any way afflicted, these too are the joys and hopes, the griefs and anxieties of the followers of Christ. Indeed, nothing genuinely human fails to raise an echo in their hearts."[27] So spoke the Fathers of the Second Vatican Council. Would that echo be absent at the heart of their liturgy?

In the case of funerals, an amplification has been provided that personalizes the memento for the dead. In Eucharistic Prayer III particularly, there is a poignant variation to which people respond sensitively. But is mourning the only situation that has a right to this special treatment?

Questions like these have come up in communities where people have made social or political commitments. In these communities, prayers linking the people's history and struggle to the history of salvation have been commonplace. "If liturgy is not about our life, it means nothing to us," these Christians say. It strikes them as something unreal.

Dom Rouillard has added up the risks and values of that way of viewing liturgy. He says: "It entails a risk of reducing the liturgy to a celebration of man — of social, political, and even revolutionary man — with a flimsy reference to Jesus Christ. But it is also a just demand for a liturgy which is no stranger to life and to the present times, concerns, and responsibilities of the Christian."[28]

In calling for a "liturgy rooted in life," some people mean a liturgy that is secular or decentralized. It is true that Vatican II recognized the "autonomy of earthly affairs" and "the legitimate autonomy of human culture."[29] But there is a trap here into which more than one pastor has fallen. Once the false "mystery," the smoke screen, of Latin was taken away, some people assumed that real participation meant centering the liturgy on the concerns of everyday life. That is a total misconception.

It is not the mystery that must come down to everyday life. It is everyday life that must enter into the Mystery.

As Father Gélineau puts it, "In the liturgy our whole human existence is engaged in our passing over to the Father, in order to be entirely condemned and entirely saved."[30]

The desire shown by charismatic groups for shared prayer

and inner experience has this basic focus. But the charismatic movement, even in its tentative groping, may be showing us something else: a legitimate need which the official liturgy is not meeting.

We must find a way to incorporate the basic cultural, scientific, social, and political realities with the responsibility each entails, into the Mystery of a creating, saving God who embraces them all.[31] We must bring these realities into our Passover, so that whoever "follows after Christ, the perfect man," becomes more of a human person.[32]

The point is not to translate liturgy into life, but life into liturgy — to involve life in its Passover into Mystery.

How do we do this? Without doubt we need to find other forms of participation, other styles of music and celebration. If we have lost some of the sacred solemnity, festive character, and harmony between song and silence, we will have to find them again. The most committed and clear-minded leaders of the reform that is now in place tell us it is capable of being perfected. Its basic direction has been traced out: life in all its dimensions lived in the fullness of the Mystery.

A thrilling task awaits us.

Notes

1. See Odo Casel, *The Mystery of Christian Worship*, Darton, Longman & Todd (London) and The Newman Press (Westminster, Maryland), 1962.
2. Pope Pius XII, *Mediator Dei et hominum*, 105 and 106.
3. *Mediator Dei*, 20.
4. *The Documents of Vatican II*, Walter M. Abbott, S.J., ed., Constitution on the Sacred Liturgy, 7.
5. *La Maison-Dieu* 1956, pages 336-338.
6. See *Mediator Dei*, 20, and Constitution on the Liturgy, 7.
7. Constitution on the Liturgy, 7.
8. Constitution on the Liturgy, 10.
9. Vatican II, Dogmatic Constitution on the Church, 11.
10. P. Jounel, "Liturgie," in the encyclopedia *Catholicisme hier, aujourd' hui, demain*, column 874.
11. P. Dominique Dye, *La Maison-Dieu* 125, 1976, page 141.

12. Adrien Nocent, O.S.B., *La messe avant et après saint Pie V,* 1977, page 63.
13. Pope Paul VI, Apostolic Constitution *Missale Romanum,* April 3, 1969.
14. *Missale Romanum,* 1969.
15. *Missale Romanum,* 1969.
16. *La Documentation Catholique,* Bayard Presse, Paris 1975, no. 1686, page 983.
17. *La Documentation Catholique,* Bayard Presse, Paris 1976, no. 1705, page 813.
18. A.-G. Martimort, *Osservatore Romano,* édition hebdomadaire en français, 10 septembre 1976, page 5.
19. P. Jounel, *La Maison-Dieu* 94, page 53.
20. *Doc. Cath.,* Paris 1975, no. 1686, page 983.
21. *Missale Romanum,* 1969.
22. Nocent, page 90.
23. Vatican II, Decree on the Missionary Activity of the Church, 8; see also 10, etc.
24. Decree on the Missionary Activity of the Church, 22.
25. Dom Ph. Rouillard, "Liturgie" in the encyclopedia *Catholicisme hier, aujourd'hui, demain,* éd. Letouzey et Ané, tome 7, Paris 1975, column 899.
26. Sacred Congregation for Divine Worship, *Liturgiae Instaurationes,* September 5, 1970.
27. Vatican II, Pastoral Constitution on the Church in the Modern World, 1.
28. Rouillard, col. 891.
29. See, for example, Dogmatic Constitution on the Church, 36 and 59.
30. Joseph Gélineau, *La Maison-Dieu* 106, 1971, page 16.
31. See Constitution on the Church in the Modern World, 43.
32. Constitution on the Church in the Modern World, 41.

Conclusion:
Pope John Paul II
on Eucharistic Renewal

How could we better crown this history of the Mass than with a text in which Pope John Paul II confirms the direction of its development? In this text, the conclusion to his letter for Holy Thursday in 1980 to the bishops of the world, entitled "The Mystery and Worship of the Holy Eucharist," the pope tells how he intends to continue the reform.

On October 17, 1978, the day after his election to the papacy, John Paul II spoke of his firm intention to implement the decisions of Vatican II. He said at that time: "We consider...our primary duty that of promoting, with prudent but encouraging action, the most exact execution of the norms and the directives of the council. Above all we favor the development of a proper mentality. First it is necessary to place oneself in harmony with the council. One must put into practice what was stated."

Then, in his Holy Thursday letter of 1980, he specified that the Yes to the Council also concerns the liturgy. He even considers liturgical reform as a *criterion* for reform of the entire life of the Church. We quote:

Permit me, venerable and dear brothers, to end these reflections of mine, which have been restricted to a detailed examination of only a few questions. In undertaking these reflections, I have had before my eyes all the work carried out by the Second Vatican Council, and have kept in mind Paul VI's encyclical Mysterium Fidei *promulgated during that council and all the documents issued after the same council for the purpose of implementing the postconciliar liturgical renewal. A* **very close and organic bond exists between the renewal of the liturgy and the renewal of the whole life of the church.**

The church not only acts but also expresses herself in the liturgy, lives by the liturgy and draws from the liturgy the strength for her life. For this reason liturgical renewal carried out correctly in the spirit of the Second Vatican Council ...

Note the phrase "carried out correctly." Some people suspected that there might be a loophole here. For example, has the Roman Missal of Paul VI been "carried out correctly"? The fact is, John Paul II quotes the new missal at least ten times in this letter. He goes on to say...

... is, in a certain sense, the measure and the condition for putting into effect the teaching of that council which we wish to accept with profound faith, convinced as we are that by means of this council the Holy Spirit "has spoken to the church" the truths and given the indications for carrying out her mission among the people of today and tomorrow.

Here John Paul II makes his first point: the directives of the Second Vatican Council, including those affecting the liturgy, will be carried out.

John Paul II had already declared that he accepts those directives. Here he confirms that by saying, *"the Holy Spirit 'has spoken to the church.'"* As far back as October 1978, he asserted that "what was 'implicit'" — in the Council — "should be made more explicit in light of experimentation that followed and in conjunction with emerging, new circumstances." In other words, he intended to nurture the seeds planted by the Council. In the letter we are reading, he reaffirms that intention in regard to the liturgy.

We shall continue in the future to take special care to promote and follow the renewal of the church according to the teaching of the Second Vatican Council, in the spirit of an ever living tradition. In fact to the substance of tradition properly understood belongs also a correct re-reading of the "signs of the times," which require us to draw from the rich treasures of revelation "things both new and old." (Mt. 13:52) Acting in this spirit, in accordance with this counsel of the Gospel, the Second Vatican Council carried out a providential effort to renew the face of the church in the sacred liturgy, most often having recourse to what is "ancient," what comes from the heritage of the fathers and is the expression of the faith and doctrine of a church which has remained united for so many centuries.

In this book we have amply emphasized Pope Paul VI's concern for "the old" in his reform. Is this the aspect John Paul II is pledging himself principally to safeguard?

In order to be able to continue in the future to put into practice the directives of the council in the field of eucharistic worship, close collaboration is necessary between the competent department of the Holy See and each episcopal conference, a collaboration which must be at the same time vigilant and creative. [So today, once more, it is a matter of "creativity."] *We must keep our sights fixed on the greatness of the most holy mystery and at the same time on spiritual movements and social changes, which are so significant for our times, since they not only sometimes create difficulties but also prepare us for a new way of participating in that great mystery of faith.*

Here now is a second point for history. Pope Pius V, the stabilizer, had his Sixtus V, the rigorist, and his Congregation of Rites which legislated in minute detail for the entire Latin Church. Pope Paul VI, the innovator, has his John Paul II, a man who believes in the importance of *"social changes"* for the liturgy. This pope dares to see in social change an opportunity for *"a new way of participating in that great mystery of faith."* With the force of authority from the *"competent department of the Holy See,"* he calls for a diversified dialogue with *"each episcopal conference"* whom he is inviting to *"creativity."*

Even if John Paul II had to authorize the public use of the missal of Pius V in certain cases for the sake of peace, this would not be an abandonment of the great innovating reform. It would be a simple application, in line with this or that episcopate, of the diversity which the reform authorizes.

The final part, coming up, raises a call for mutual understanding. It is the historic vocation of the Eucharist to be a *"focal point and constitutive center"* for the Church. The word *unity* is repeated or paraphrased as many as seven times in these final paragraphs. The variety of rites is no danger to unity. This is evident from the fact that this letter is addressed to the bishops of the entire Catholic Church, including those of Eastern rites.

> *Above all, I wish to emphasize that the problems of the liturgy, and in particular of the eucharistic liturgy, must not be an occasion for dividing Catholics and for threatening the unity of the church. This is demanded by an elementary understanding of that sacrament which Christ has left us as the source of spiritual unity.* [These words appear to be for the benefit of people who have only a rudimentary understanding of what Eucharist and Church are about.] *And how could the eucharist, which in the church is the* sacramentum pietatis, signum unitatis vinculum caritatis [sacrament of piety, sign of unity, bond of love, *ed.*], *form between us at this time a point of division and a source of distortion of thought and behavior, instead of being the focal point and constitutive center, which it truly is in its essence, of the unity of the church itself?*

Here, in the following lines, the author of *Redemptor Hominis* is a moving advocate of unity.

> *We are all equally indebted to our Redeemer. We should all listen together to that Spirit of truth and of life whom he has promised to the church and who is operative in her. In the name of this truth and of this love, in*

the name of the crucified Christ and of his mother, I ask you, and beg you: Let us abandon all opposition and division, and let us all unite in this great mission of salvation which is the price and at the same time the fruit of our redemption. The Apostolic See will continue to do all that is possible to provide the means of ensuring that unity of which we speak. Let everyone avoid anything in his own way of acting which could "grieve the Holy Spirit." (Eph. 4:30)

The second last sentence above expresses the lengths to which the Holy See will go toward *"ensuring that unity."* Here is one of the great lessons of history: if maintaining peace is proper to ecumenical dialogue — which is what the last part of the following paragraph seems to be getting at — perhaps maintaining *"collegial unity"* among bishops can go even beyond that and become communion *"in the light of the Holy Spirit."*

In order that this unity and the constant and systematic collaboration which leads to it may be perseveringly continued, I beg on my knees that, through the intercession of Mary, holy spouse of the Holy Spirit and mother of the church, we may all receive the light of the Holy Spirit. And blessing everyone, with all my heart I once more address myself to you, my venerable brothers in the episcopate, with a fraternal greeting and with full trust. In this collegial unity in which we share, let us do all we can to ensure that the eucharist may become an ever greater source of life and light for the conscience of all our brothers and sisters of all the communities in the universal unity of Christ's church on earth.

Then follow the apostolic blessing and the date, February 24, 1980.

The history of the Mass goes on, more alive than ever. It is the history of our one yet varied response to that unique call: *"Do this in memory of me."*

Index of Names and Subjects

A

Adaptation, liturgical, 118
Adrian I, Pope, 70-71
Africa, Church of North, 39, 44, 51, 61
Agape, 30, 31
Alcuin, 70-72, 73, 76; Supplement of, 71
Allegory, 81, 83
Altar, 73, 82-83, 86
Ambrose, St., 46, 48, 49, 61, 121
Anicetus, Pope, 36, 42
Apostles, 9-14 *passim,* 18-28 *passim*
Apostolic Tradition of St. Hippolytus, 37-39, 41
Aquinas, St. Thomas, 81, 83
Aramaic, 12, 22-23
Arianism, 45, 63, 71
Augustine, St., 44, 46, 48, 61

B

Baptism (required for participation in Eucharist), 21, 31
Beauduin, Lambert, O.S.B., 114
Bell, 74, 85
Benedict, St., 52
Benediction of the Blessed Sacrament, 103

Bishop, liturgical role of, 32-33
Body and Blood of Christ, 13-14
Botte, Bernard, O.S.B., 119
Bouyer, Louis, 119
Bread, and wine, 24; breaking of, 19, 21, 23-24; consecrated and reserved for next day's Mass, 42; unleavened, 26, 73
Burchard, John, 98

C

Cabrol, Dom, O.S.B., 56, 57, 112
Callistus, Pope St., 37, 40, 42, 79, 92, 111, 117
Canon (anaphora), Ambrosian, 61; meaning of term, 53; new, 120-122; Roman, 49, 61, 65, 71
Casel, Odo, O.S.B., 114, 131
Chant, Gregorian, 48, 71, 81, 86, 108, 110, 127
Charlemagne, Emperor, 67, 69-71, 75-77, 87, 117, 125
Chasuble, 74, 86
Choir, 54, 86, 107
Clement of Rome, Pope St., 32-33
Communion, after Mass, 106; as Viaticum, 85; at papal Mass, 55; frequent and daily,

113-114; from the cup, 55; in early Church, 41-42; in the hand, 73; infrequent, 73, 85, 106; on the tongue, 73; reserved for next day's Mass, 42; rite for the sick, 85, 98-99; sent by pope to other bishops, 42; standing and kneeling, 42, 73; taken home by people, 42; under both species, 73, 85, 119

Communion rail, 73, 85

Concelebration, 115, 119

Congregation of Rites, 102-103, 111

Constitution on the Sacred Liturgy, 115, 116, 117, 118-119, 131

Controversies, liturgical, 29-43 *passim*

Covenant, 13-14, 25

Creativity, liturgical, 40-41

D

Decree on the Missionary Activity of the Church, 117, 132

Didache, the, 30-32

Divinity of Christ, doctrine of and liturgy, 45, 63

E

Easter, celebration of, 56; controversy over the date of, 35-37

Eucharist (meaning of term), 25

Experiments, liturgical, 118

F

Filioque (in the Creed), 77

G

Gelasius, Pope, 52, 66

Gélineau, Joseph, 119, 130, 132

Genuflecting, 63, 73, 83

Gestures, repetition of, 73, 82-83, 98

Greek as language of liturgy, 12, 22-23, 37, 39-40, 42, 43, 117

Gregory the Great, Pope St., 45, 46, 52; and Gregorian chant, 48; liturgical reform of, 51-52

Guéranger, Prosper, O.S.B., 110

H

Hellriegel, Martin, 114

Henry II, Emperor St., 77, 81

Hippolytus of Rome, St., 117; *Apostolic Tradition* of — *see Apostolic Tradition;* opponent of Latin in liturgy, 37, 40, 42-43

Hoeffner, Cardinal Joseph, 123, 124

Host, desire to see, 73, 83-85; shape and size of, 64, 73

I

Ignatius of Antioch, St., 33

Improvisation, liturgical, 40
Irenaeus of Lyons, St., 36-37, 42

J

Jesus, 9-14 *passim*, 18-20
John XXIII, Pope, 109, 113
John Paul II, Pope, 133-137
Jounel, Pierre, 14, 15, 119, 123, 131
Jungmann, Josef A., S.J., 9, 15, 46, 57, 68, 73, 87, 97, 99, 100, 105, 111, 112
Justin Martyr, St., *First Apology of*, 34-35

L

La Maison-Dieu, 15, 27, 115, 131, 132
Language(s), intelligible (understandable), 23, 79-80; liturgical, 22-23, 79-80; mother tongue, 12, 22, 117; mysterious, 22; vernacular, 93, 105, 117, 129
Last Supper, 9-14 *passim*, 24
Latin as language of liturgy, 39-40, 79, 117, 128, 130
LeBrun, Pierre, 105
Leclerc, H., 14
Lectionary of Pius V, 98
Lefebvre, Dom, O.S.B., 114
Leo XIII, Pope, 108
Leo the Great, Pope St., 45, 46, 51, 66
Libelli (little books), 49, 66
Liturgies (liturgical families),

Ambrosian (Milanese), 46, 51, 61; Armenian, 50; Byzantine (Greek, of St. John Chrysostom), 46, 50, 123, 124; Celtic, 51, 61-62; Chaldean, 50; Coptic, 50; Ethiopian, 50; Gallican, 51, 61-65, 68, 78, 123; Georgian, 50; Gothic (Visigoth, Mozarabic, Spanish), 51, 62; Malabar, 50; Maronite, 50, 123; Roman, 51, 56-57, 68; Syriac, 50; Ukrainian (Ruthenian), 50
Luther, Martin, 81, 91-92, 95

M

Martimort, A.-G., 43, 87, 100, 123, 132
Mass of the Roman Rite, The (Jungmann), 9, 15, 57, 68, 80, 87, 100, 111
Mass, as a memorial (remembrance), 9, 13, 23, 25, 39, 92; doctrine of Trent regarding, 92-93; for the dead, 82, 86; Franco-German, 75, 87; Franco-Roman, 72-75; German *Singmesse*, 108; in early Christianity, 18-27, 29-43, 44-57; in the home, 30, 41; in the Middle Ages, 60-68, 69-80, 81-87; in the modern era, 90-99, 101-111, 113-131; in the time of the apostles, 18-27; in the time of the persecutions, 29-43; low, 82, 106, 108; Luther's view regarding, 91-92; meaning of

term, 9, 53, 86; of Christ, 9-14; of Pius v, 90-111 *passim;* papal (of Gregory the Great), 53-56; parts of (particular) — *see* Parts and Prayers of the Mass; prayers of (particular) — *see* Parts and Prayers of the Mass; prayers of (in singular and plural), 72-73; private, 75, 92; sanctoral, 52, 124; solemn, 82; structure of, 24-26; Sunday, 75, 78; sung (chanted), 86, 107-108; superstitions (deviations) regarding, 81, 82, 91; temporal, 52, 124; votive, 52, 82, 124; with Blessed Sacraments exposed, 85

Meal, domestic, 24; Eucharist as, 24, 25; Passover and Jewish, 10, 18, 25, 26, 124; sacrificial, 24, 26

Mediator Dei (encyclical letter), 114, 131

Missal, forerunner of, 52; Franco-Germanic, 74-75; Gallican, 67; of Pius v, 95-99, 101-102, 108-109, 117; of the Roman Curia, 95, 97, 99; of Paul vi (post-Vatican ii), 68, 113-131 *passim*

Missale Romanum (apostolic constitution), 119, 120-122

Music, liturgical, 47-48, 86, 107-108, 114, 128, 131

Mystery, 14, 129-131

Mystical Body of Christ (encyclical *Mystici Corporis*), 114

N

New Testament, 9-14 *passim*

Nocent, Adrien, O.S.B., 98, 100, 112, 120

O

On the Sacraments *(De Sacramentis),* 49, 57

Organ, 74, 86, 107

P

Parsch, Pius, 114

Participation of the faithful, 35, 66, 71, 107, 111, 115-117, 130

Parts and Prayers of the Mass, *Agnus Dei,* 55, 85, 86, 107; *Amen,* 35, 49; Canon, 55, 65; collection (offerings), 35, 41, 63; Communion — *see* Communion; *Confiteor,* 85, 99; consecration, 14, 24, 84; Creed, Nicene *(Credo),* 75-77, 81, 107; elevation of the chalice, 84, 95; of the host, 84-85, 95; Epistle, 40, 54, 82, 108, 124; Eucharistic Prayer, 49, 120-121, 129; Eucharistic Prayer i, 49, 121-122, 128; Eucharistic Prayer ii, 37, 122-123; Eucharistic Prayer iii, 123, 130; Eucharistic Prayer iv, 124; *Gloria in excelsis,* 54, 86, 96; Gospel, 40, 55, 83, 124; Holy, Holy, Holy *(Sanctus),* 24, 38,

55, 63, 71, 86, 107; Homily
(preaching), 106, 119; *Introit,*
54; *Ite missa est,* 53, 56, 95;
Kiss of peace, 34, 41, 54, 55,
64, 76; *Kyrie eleison,* 54, 63,
86, 107; Last Gospel, 120;
Liturgy of the Eucharist,
25-26, 33, 34, 35; Liturgy of
the Word (memoirs), 24-25,
34, 35; *Libera nos,* 55; *Memento* for the Church, 31; for
the living, 31; Offertory
(Preparation of Gifts), 34, 35,
55, 98, 107, 120; *Pater Noster,* 55, 107; *Per ipsum,* 55,
85; *Placeat,* 96; Prayer of the
Faithful (Common Prayer),
35, 119; Prayers after Mass,
108; Preface, 55, 64, 107,
120; Preparation of the Gifts
— *see* Offertory above; *Sanctus* — *see* Holy, Holy, Holy
above
Paul VI, Pope, 14, 37, 49,
113-131 *passim*
*Paul, St. (Saul), 11-14
passim*, 18-25 *passim*
Pentecost, 18, 27, 79, 111,
129
Pius V, Pope St., 14, 90-99
passim, 121, 125
Pius X, Pope St., 109, 113
Pius XII, Pope St., 109, 114,
126, 131
Polycarp, St., 36, 42
Preface of the Blessed Trinity,
108
Priest (presbyter), location of
at Mass, 41, 73, 82, 83; role

of in liturgy, 32-33
Pulpit, 106

R

Real Presence in Blessed Sacrament, 83-85, 92, 106, 115
Regulation, liturgical, 118
Reinhold, H. A., 114
Rouillard, Dom, O.S.B.,
128, 130, 132
Rubricians and rubrics, 81,
83, 98, 103-104, 108, 109,
117

S

Sabbath (Saturday), 19, 22, 27
Sacramentary, Ancient Gela-
sian, 66-67, 71; Gregorian,
67; *Hadrianum,* 67, 71-72;
Leonine (of Verona), 66, 67;
Paduan *(Paduense),* 67, 70;
Recent Gelasian, 67, 70,
71-72; Roman, 65-68
Sacrifice, Christian, and
human sacrifice, 29, 34; as a
meal, 24, 26; Christian liturgy
as, 22; of the Cross, 22, 92
Sacrifice, Jewish, as a meal,
26; in the Temple, 21
Sanctuary, 54, 73, 107
Sixtus V, Pope, 102, 103, 111
Solemnes, Abbey of, 110
Spirit, Holy, 14, 18, 22, 27,
123
Sunday, 22, 27, 34, 36
Synagogue, 18, 20, 21, 24,
124

T

Temple of Jerusalem, 19-25
passim
Thanksgiving, Eucharist as,
25, 31, 33, 38, 39
Trent, Council of, 91, 92-94,
96, 101, 107, 113, 119, 126
Trinity, doctrine of and liturgy, 63, 64, 77

V

Vagaggini, Cyprian, O.S.B.,
119, 123
Vatican II, liturgical reform
of, 29, 113-131 *passim*
Vestments, 41, 47, 74, 86
Victor, Pope, 36, 42

W

Worship (Orate, Fratres)
magazine, 114

Y

Year (cycle, liturgical), 82,
115, 119, 124

Z

Zebah Todah, 25-26